PHOTOGRAPHY
FOR THE JOY OF IT

P9-DDH-089

FREEMAN PATTERSON

SIERRA CLUB BOOKS
SAN FRANCISCO

The Sierra Club, founded in 1892 by John Muir, has devoted itself to the study and protection of the earth's scenic and ecological resources – mountains, wetlands, woodlands, wild shores and rivers, deserts and plains. The publishing program of the Sierra Club offers books to the public as a nonprofit educational service in the hope that they may enlarge the public's understanding of the Club's basic concerns. The point of view expressed in each book, however, does not necessarily represent that of the Club. The Sierra Club has some sixty chapters coast to coast, in Canada, Hawaii, and Alaska. For information about how you may participate in its programs to preserve wilderness and the quality of life, please address inquiries to Sierra Club, 730 Polk Street, San Francisco, CA 94109.

Copyright © 1989 by Key Porter Books Limited.

All rights reserved under International and Pan-American Copyright Conventions. No part of this book may be reproduced in any form or by any electronic or mechanical means, including information storage and retrieval systems, without permission in writing from the publisher.

Library of Congress Cataloging-in-Publication Data

Patterson, Freeman, 1937-
  Photography for the joy of it / Freeman Patterson.
    p.   cm.
  Reprint. Originally published: Toronto; New York: Van Nostrand, 1977.
  Includes index.
  ISBN 0-87156-697-4
  1. Photography.   I. Title.
  TR145.P33 1989
  770—dc 19   88-30837
                                               CIP

Typesetting by Imprint Typesetting
Colour separations by Herzig Somerville Limited
All photographs are by the author.

10   9   8   7   6   5   4   3   2   1

Printed and bound in Canada

Contents

Preface to the revised edition

For me the joy of photography lies in being at ease with my camera, being keenly aware of things around me, and feeling free to photograph them as I please. It's not in being restricted by rules or formulas, by equipment or technical considerations, by subject matter or type of film, or other photographers and their work. It's in being myself and in making photographs that communicate what I see and what I feel about what I see. It's also in being disciplined – being thoughtful about what I do so that I capture the images I want. After more than twenty-five years as an amateur and professional photographer, I am even more convinced that fine images don't happen, they are made – and made very carefully. Using my camera regularly and analysing what I am doing and why has made photography a deeply satisfying, creative adventure.

However, this book is for *you* – whether you have only a basic knowledge of camera operation or have been making fine images for many years. It's about learning to "see" – learning to be aware of things around you, seeing things you have never noticed before, using your eyes all the time, not just when you pick up your camera. It's about being conscious of your subject matter and your treatment of it – and what it means to you and those who view your pictures of it. It's also about improving your ability to make the pictures you want. Although the technical references are to 35mm single-lens reflex cameras, the book is also for photographers who own other camera systems. It's for the colour photographer and the black-and-white photographer, the photographer of nature, architecture, people, the old and the young. It's for everyone who wants to photograph – for the joy of it!

In this revised edition, I have updated the chapter on cameras, lenses, and other equipment to reflect advances in technology. However, I've been careful to retain all the information that has not changed. Those ideas are as important today as they ever were. The rest of the book contains minor alterations – a few words here, a sentence or two there – in order to make a point more clearly or to reflect progression in my own thinking.

   I am grateful to the thousands of readers and workshop students who, over the years, have communicated their positive responses to the original edition and who, in this way, have encouraged me to make only necessary changes to the text. Readers of this edition will benefit from their experience and input. Also, I want to express very special appreciation to my editor, Susan Kiil, who first worked with me on the original edition of *Photography for the Joy of It* and has since guided me through the preparation of my other books.

Freeman Patterson
Shampers Bluff
New Brunswick
March 1989

Photography for the joy of it

In making photographs, two things are important above all others – the subject matter and you. Photographs are what happen when you and the subject meet, and you use a camera to describe the meeting. A photograph is a visual description of the relationship between the subject and the photographer; and a good photograph is one which clearly shows the character of the subject while revealing the photographer's response to it.

If you think of a photograph in this way, you'll find your personal direction as a photographer emerging and becoming clearer. Sometimes it takes a while to understand what's happening, and to decide upon what you expect from the relationship. Good relationships require a lot of give and take, and a lot of hard work. But the process of coming to know yourself through interaction with someone or something else is very satisfying. In the end, you get the picture – of both of you.

In some photographs the subject is everything and the photographer's task is to reveal its essence as accurately as possible. The photographer must struggle to keep his own preconceptions from obscuring the truth.

In other pictures the subject is unimportant in itself, but is important as a symbol or a tool for revealing how the photographer thinks and feels. In these images, subject matter is like potter's clay – you mold it however you want.

You probably tend to lean in one direction sometimes and in the other direction just as often – probably without ever thinking much about it. You occupy a middle ground, which is not a bad place to be, but your photographic point of view does need to be examined if you want to achieve results which satisfy you. So, let's talk about the importance of the subject and about the importance of the photographer as a person.

The subject. Many people enjoy photographing objects and situations created by nature – landscapes, flowers and trees, insects and animals. When they approach these subjects as natural historians, their aim is to photograph them with as much authenticity as possible. If they find a *Russula* mushroom growing at the edge of a forest, they wouldn't think of transplanting it to a nearby meadow, just because there's more light there or because they like the grasses a lot better than the tangled underbrush. They know that the normal habitat of this particular mushroom is essential to the mushroom's existence, and that all the characteristics of a *Russula* – size, shape, colour – depend on its growing where it does. So they make the subject, a mushroom and its setting, paramount, and pay careful attention to technical adjustments. Will Fujichrome give more accurate colour than Kodachrome? Will a lower angle show the gills of the mushroom better? Should the picture include a little more habitat in order to show the ecological conditions necessary for a *Russula*'s growth? In all these ways they are looking for and trying to photograph the truth.

All of this is fairly easy to do with nature, but a lot harder to do with other subjects. Take people, for example. You can be fairly detached about a mushroom, but you probably will find it almost impossible to be neutral about a wildly happy child or a stumbling drunk. Your personal experiences and emotions tend to blur your objectivity. You are interpreting the subject and the situation from the moment you see it. And, if you are to photograph the subject at all, you must respond quickly. There isn't time for analysis. You make the picture, and what you get is an image that not only communicates vividly about the subject but also tells something of who you are – only you would have taken that picture in that way.

So, the photographer also matters. Your reaction to a subject determines the setting of the image – the subject's environment. The camera looks both ways. A photograph is usually as good a description of who's behind the lens as who or what is in front of it.

The photographer as a person. Nobody can ever hide behind a camera. Accept the fact that when you make pictures you are revealing a lot about yourself. For me, most subjects have symbolic importance and I am free to approach them as I want in order to make a visual statement. You will produce your best images when you know what your feelings are and choose a compatible subject through which to express them. If you feel hope and joy, and convey these through the bouncing light and delicate colours of a summer sunrise, you are probably choosing a subject that is compatible with your emotions, one which stimulates them.

However, if you employ pure technique (such as pure design, deliberate underexposure or tinting with food colours) with little regard for the nature of your subject matter, you may end up producing pictures that lack harmony. The content and style of a picture must work together in order to convey feelings and ideas effectively.

Sorting out your thoughts and emotions isn't always easy. There are times when you want to experience the release which photography brings, but nothing seems to work. You have trouble even finding things to photograph. This is a fairly common experience, and it usually occurs when you're tense, unhappy with yourself, or worried. Part of your mind is on photography, and part of it is somewhere else.

The trick is to concentrate on your photography, not on your problems. Stop. Try to identify what you want to shoot. If you can't make up your mind, start with a simple exercise in composition on whatever material is available. Instead of looking for a masterpiece, start exploring the facade of the nearest building, or studying the arrangements of books on your shelves. Try things you can cope with

11

– technically and emotionally. Save the analysis of what you're doing – and your masterpieces – for another day. The chances are that by using photography as a form of therapy, you'll feel better. You'll keep your technical skills sharpened, and you may end up making some excellent pictures too.

At other times, everything is right. You're ready to accept the challenge of photographing what moves you. Your senses are keen, and you feel that a good experience is about to happen. As you move along the street you spot a wild configuration of shapes and colours reflected in a window. This is the place!

If you're going to do the subject matter and yourself justice, the first question you must ask yourself is "Why did I stop here?" Zero in on your motivation. Identify what's exciting you as quickly as you can. What do the shapes and colours suggest to you? What do they symbolize? Or, are you simply intrigued by the intricate blendings of tones and hues? If you can put your finger on your personal motivation, then you are in a strong position to ask yourself the right questions about technique. In photography, as in just about everything else, knowing why you are doing something will help you do it well.

In many situations, of course, you won't have time for reflection. You'll have to act – fast! But afterward, when you see your images, ask the same questions. Picture evaluation is much more than deciding whether or not you used the right lens or exposure; it's deciding if the image you made accurately represents how you felt at the time you made it. Useful evaluation means looking at yourself as well as at your photographs.

Making photographs aids the process of self-discovery. Studying your images helps it further. A happy sort of spiral commences, and continues as long as you make pictures regularly. The more images you make thoughtfully, the better you know yourself; the better you know yourself, the more likely you are to make pictures which satisfy you.

It's very important to *be yourself* when you are making photographs. Try to learn from others without letting them direct your interests or cloud your personal vision. A good teacher will not try to force you in any particular direction, and a good student will not follow even the best instructor like a sheep. Plot your own directions and follow them.

Whether you are documenting subjects which are important to you, or using them as vehicles to express your own ideas and feelings, do your photography *for the joy of it*! There's no better reason for making pictures.

Most of us get started in photography because we're excited by pictures, especially by pictures we discover by ourselves. Really "seeing" things is important to us, and photographs are a way of preserving what we see and of sharing it with others.

Photography is a chance to recapture the profound sense of excitement, the magic of living, which we felt so strongly as children. Photography is a way to yell "Whoopee!" again and really mean it. It offers us opportunities to be creative in ways we like, and a chance to let go. This book is for all of you who make pictures for the sheer joy of it!

I use the term "make pictures" deliberately, because people who love photography don't simply lift a camera to their eye and press the shutter release. You don't just "take" pictures. You do more than that, much more. You become involved with what you're photographing, and because you're involved, you think a lot about what you're doing. You want to express the subject and your feelings about it accurately. So you care about your workmanship.

Caring and joy go together. In photography as in anything else, you'll seldom find one without the other.

I can't remember when my desire to make photographs germinated. A rather nebulous but quietly incessant urge has always been with me. Since I couldn't afford a camera until I was almost twenty, I had to "make photographs" in other ways. So I just used my eyes. I noticed things. I looked at them carefully, especially things I liked.

Among the things I liked best were plants, particularly wildflowers and trees. I didn't care much for vegetables, because they grew in long rows full of weeds where I'd have to labour for days on end. Vegetables were controlled, but flowers and trees were free.

I couldn't "discover" carrots, because I knew exactly where my father and I had planted the seeds. Besides, I found them boring because they were so purely practical. But wildflowers were another matter. To find a rhododendron bush blooming in a clump of cedars was a surprise, an unexpected thrill! I felt that somehow the wildflowers were blooming for me, and that if I didn't look for them and find them, their supreme act of beauty would be lost.

I feel the same way about visual images. All around me all the time are pictures waiting to be discovered. Making a photograph is the act of giving permanence to something transient. It's making sure the wildflowers will never go away.

Photographers talk about "creating" images, but I'm not certain that anybody has ever created anything with a camera. Perhaps it is more accurate to say that God creates, and that some human beings discover. Discovery is not accidental. We discover only when we make ourselves ready to receive.

Some photographers seek discovery by mastering the machinery of the craft: cameras, lenses, films, lighting, exposure, and design are their primary concerns. But I think photography begins somewhere else.

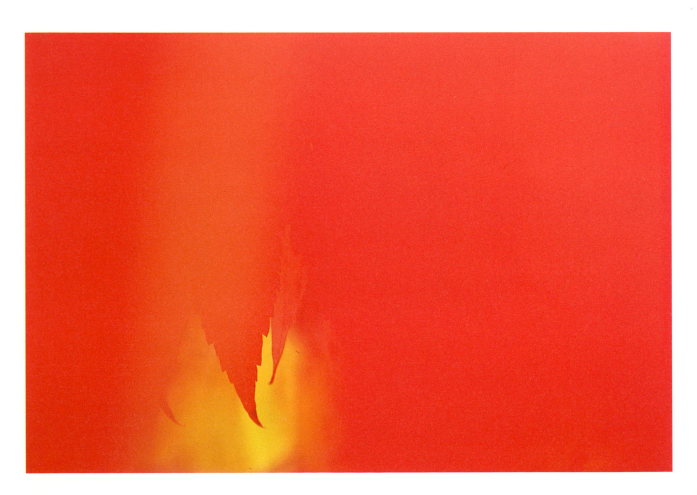

It begins with wildflowers, or kids, or sunrises, or motorcycle gangs, or gothic cathedrals, or falling in love, or growing old. It begins with the things that matter to you. And it ends, with visual statements that express what matters to you about these things. The cameras and films are merely tools.

The best photographs are those which have a clear purpose that is well expressed. But some photographs transcend both clear purpose and good expression; they move beyond competence and become art.

Photography is both documentary – recording wildflowers, people, architecture; and interpretative – the same subjects, but capturing personal insights along with outward appearances. Good documentary photographers can capture the event, with fairness, and at the same time communicate their deep interest in it. Their respect for and involvement with their chosen material brings tremendous challenges, because they must be honest and objective about their subjects.

It's exciting to view the work of photographers whose understanding of a subject and whose skill with the tools and techniques result in images which go beyond purely physical description and reveal the character and spirit of what is being photographed.

The environments in which photographers work are important – try to discover the ones which excite you. Your emotional response to the situation will be expressed in the pictures you make.

Older photographers who have cared about their favourite subject matter for many years almost seem to have a capacity for astral projection into their most cherished environment. Young people dream dreams. Older people have followed their dreams, and because they have direction they are often able to produce effective images consistently. Nothing gives me more pleasure than seeing an older person probing the boundaries, testing the limits, and relishing the familiar sights of his or her personal landscape. Their experience of joy gains in intensity because it is full of so many familiar paths and pleasant digressions.

For everybody, photography is an opportunity to discover personal paths and to follow those which promise excitement and pleasure. You can wander at your own pace, pause to appreciate each new discovery and move on at will. Photography is a way to explore your world and yourself. You may answer the call of your own spirit. You are free. If you learn to see well and to use your tools effectively, your photographs will be unique, personal expressions, images which bring you joy in the making – and in the sharing with other people.

Choosing your tools

Cameras, lenses, and other equipment

If you've purchased this book, you probably have a camera and other photographic equipment and use it a lot. But, if you don't own a camera, or if you are looking for better equipment, here are some suggestions for you. Most of these refer to the 35mm single-lens reflex camera, the type I use. Its features allow for the greatest freedom and ease of experimentation, with the fewest technical considerations and calculations. However, other types of cameras produce excellent images, and you may prefer one of them.

1 / Think of your shopping around as an opportunity for learning. Study brochures on different brands of cameras and equipment and ask your photographic friends or dealer to explain anything you don't understand. If possible, try out the models which interest you most – even if it means shooting a roll of film at a friend's home or right in the camera store. You can't get "the feel" of equipment by reading about it. Whatever you do, don't hurry. Be methodical. Satisfy yourself before you buy that you are getting what you want.

2 / Buy from a reputable dealer, especially one who is not given to high-pressure salesmanship. You have a lot to gain by dealing with and being thoughtful of an honest and considerate businessperson, even if his prices on cameras, lenses, and other equipment are somewhat higher than they are down the street. Believe me, that kind of interest is worth the extra money in the long run.

Cameras
There are many important items to consider when you are choosing a camera. These include:

1 / *The total camera system.* Is there a variety of lenses and other equipment available for the camera model you are considering? Think carefully of your long-term needs at this stage.

2 / *The camera's weight.* If you expect to carry your camera and other equipment for more than a few minutes at a time, or intend to use it on long trips, consider its weight carefully. If two models seem equally good, you could be wise to get the lighter one.

3 / *The lens.* 35mm cameras are almost invariably offered for sale with 50 or 55mm lenses. These are called "standard" lenses, and are presumed to be what most people want, at least for their first lens. But you may not want a standard lens. If not, buy only the camera body, and purchase the lens you want to take the place of the standard one. (For a discussion of different lenses, see pages 29 to 33).

Many cameras now accept only lenses that can focus automatically. Auto focusing is a definite convenience for tracking moving objects and for many difficult lighting situations. However, some brands offer more accurate or user-friendly automatic focusing than others. It's a good idea to make comparisons. Also, since there will be times when you want to focus manually (because you disagree with the lens' point of focus), make sure you can easily disengage the automatic feature. Even with the most highly sophisticated and versatile auto-focus system, you may occasionally want or need manual operation.

4 / *The exposure system.* These days virtually all 35mm single-lens reflex cameras have electronic shutters, and more and more can be operated in one of four possible modes – manual, aperture-preferred, shutter-preferred, and program. In the manual mode, you choose both the aperture (lens opening) and the shutter speed you want; in the aperture-preferred mode, you select the lens opening and the camera automatically chooses the shutter speed required for correct exposure; in the shutter-preferred mode, you select the shutter speed and the camera chooses the lens opening; in the program mode, the camera chooses both lens opening and shutter speed, usually on the basis of the focal length of the lens you are using. In all three of the automatic modes, you can override the camera's decision (that is, overexpose or underexpose) by pressing an override lever or button. Since all these exposure-system features are readily available, it's important to compare camera brands and models to find out which camera is best designed for your use.

Also, today's cameras are likely to provide for automatic exposure with flash – a very useful feature for situations when there is low light or the need for "fill-in" light to reduce contrast. Again, make comparisons by examining various models of cameras and studying their instruction manuals. Can you switch to fully manual flash, if you want? Is sequence flash possible for action photography? The manuals will help you to ask and answer these and other questions.

The exposure system depends, of course, on the camera meter. (For a full discussion of meters and their use, see the chapter entitled "Exposure.") When you are contemplating a camera purchase, find out if the meter reads the light reflected from the entire picture area, or from just one spot, or from several key spots. Check to see if you can change from one area of measurement to another. For example, can you switch from an overall light reading to a spot measurement? This can be of great assistance in many situations, especially when the most important object in your picture is darker or lighter than everything else and you want to make sure you expose it accurately.

5 / *Viewfinder screens, or viewing screens.* If you have difficulty focusing properly when you look through the viewfinder, check other viewing screens available for that camera model. If there are no other screens available, don't buy the camera.

6 / *Depth-of-field preview button.* Every serious amateur will want to select the correct depth of field for every picture he makes. Make sure that the model you buy has a depth-of-field preview button or lever, and if it doesn't, check to see if such a button or lever is on the lenses made for that camera model.

7 / *Double exposures and multiple exposures.* Consult the instruction manual or the dealer to find out whether or not you can make double or multiple exposures with the camera you are considering. Ask for a demonstration.

8 / *Self-timer or exposure-delay lever.* Most cameras have a lever which can delay the exposure for up to 15 seconds from the moment you press the shutter release. This device will be important to you when you have your camera on a tripod and you want to get into the picture yourself. It's also useful when you don't have a cable release to prevent the tripod and camera from jiggling during an exposure. You can activate the self-timer, step back, and the exposure will be made a few seconds later.

9 / *The price.* All brand-name cameras are carefully manufactured. Unless you require the ultimate in workmanship, there may be no good reason to buy a $1000 camera, if a $500 model has most of the same features. Very expensive cameras may have lenses which produce sharper photographs than less expensive cameras. However, if you expect to shoot mostly slides and project them, the value and effect of the extra sharpness will be reduced, because projector lenses do not match the quality of camera lenses.

Be cautious about buying a very expensive camera at a greatly reduced price – you may later find that extra lenses and equipment are not a bargain at all. A model offered at a substantially reduced price may be one which is going off the market, which could mean that in a few years parts and service may be hard to find. Most manufacturers service old models for many years, so this may not be a major consideration. However, it's still worthwhile to check whether the dealer has several brands of cameras on sale, several models of one brand, or just this one model. If only one model is on sale, ask some pointed questions.

10 / *The manufacturer's guarantee and service.* Your camera should be covered by at least a two-year warranty against mechanical defects. It's important to inquire from friends and your dealer about the speed and quality of service available for the camera you are considering. What's the point of owning a camera which takes two months to have repaired?

Lenses

There are many different kinds of lenses available for 35mm cameras, but most photographers speak of four general types or "focal lengths" – standard, wide-angle, telephoto, and zoom lenses. (For a discussion of macro and macro-zoom lenses, see pages 38 and 39.)

Kinds of lenses. The focal length of a *standard lens* is roughly equivalent to the diagonal of the negative. For 35mm cameras, a standard lens is usually 50 or 55mm in focal length, and produces pictures in natural, realistic perspective.

At the same distance from the subject, a *wide-angle lens* (35, 28, 24, 21, or 17mm, for example) produces a smaller image of the subject on the same area of film as a standard lens, but it covers a larger field of view than a standard lens. The shorter the focal length of the lens, the smaller the subject image will be, but the wider the field of view will be. At the same distance a 25mm lens will produce a subject image approximately half the size of that produced by a 50mm lens, but it will cover twice the field of view.

At the same distance from the subject, a *telephoto* or *long-focus lens* (100, 135, 200, 300, 500, or 1000mm, for example) produces a larger image of the subject on the same area of film as the standard lens, but it covers a narrower field of view. The longer the focal length of the lens, the larger the subject image will be, and the narrower the field of view will be. At the same distance a 100mm lens will produce a subject image approximately twice as large as that produced by a 50mm lens, but will cover only half the field of view.

Lenses with a variable focal length are known as *zoom lenses*. For example, an 80 - 200mm zoom can be set at 80mm, 200mm, or at any focal length between.

The focal length of a lens influences its depth of field. Depth of field is the span of distance in your picture which appears fully sharp. (See also "Point of focus and depth of field," page 97.) A wide-angle (short focal length) lens gives greater depth of field than a standard lens, and a standard lens gives more than a telephoto (long focal length) lens. The shorter the focal length the greater the depth of field; the longer the focal length, the less the depth of field. An 80 - 200mm zoom lens will show considerably greater depth of field at 80mm than it will at 200mm.

Uses of lenses. Lenses of different focal lengths and especially zoom lenses give a photographer much greater control over the scale of his subject matter and over apparent perspective. Consequently, lenses play a fundamental role in the composition of photographs. Let's consider some ways to use the different lenses well.

The secret of using a *wide-angle lens* effectively lies in paying attention to the foreground of the composition. A strong foreground object, relatively large in the composition, helps the viewer to judge the scale of the other objects in the picture. Neglect the foreground, and you are usually in trouble when you compose with lenses from 17 to 35mm.

Wide-angle lenses are usually used to best advantage when you hold your camera vertically. This reduces the picture's width, but produces a tremendous sense of depth. In the Rockies, for example, try positioning the camera vertically and including a stream, a rock, or a clump of alpine flowers in the immediate foreground, and let the rest of the picture sweep away to the towering peaks.

When you use a wide-angle lens for a landscape, don't be afraid to move in very close to the foreground object. Try tilting the camera down to provide a little space underneath the foreground object, then inching it up again to include just a "sliver" of sky, as I did in the photograph on page 151. On the other hand, by tilting the camera up toward the sky and retaining only a small amount of land at the base of the picture area, you can also produce a striking sense of space.

There are two other uses for wide-angle lenses. First, if you want to reduce the size or impact of a secondary object in the composition, use a wide-angle lens and position yourself close to the main subject. Second, if you want to show the main subject of your composition in a typical environment (for example, the mayor in front of the city hall, or animals in their natural habitat) a wide-angle lens can be valuable. Moving close to your subject will give it prominence, and at the same time will capture a large part of the setting. Your picture will tell a story neatly and quickly.

Use your wide-angle lens courageously. Capitalize on its unique characteristics. Avoid thinking of it as a lens which will merely include more things in your picture. Wide-angle lenses of 24 or 28mm are sensible choices for many photographers. A 35mm may be too close to the 50mm standard lens for your taste, and a 17mm may create visual distortion which you don't like.

A *telephoto lens* compresses distance and diminishes apparent perspective, introducing new visual elements into a composition. Chief among these is the close grouping of objects which are actually far apart. Also, because a long lens has a narrower field of view than a standard lens, it leads to simpler design. The number of visual components is reduced. These factors, along with shallower depth of field than a standard lens, mean that a long lens forces you to see differently.

For example, a telephoto lens enables you to shoot *through* foreground material, such as grasses or wire fences, showing them as vague forms at maximum apertures (such as f/3.5) and sometimes eliminating them altogether. The shallow depth of field which causes objects near the lens to be out of focus can be used effectively in visual design. If you poke a long lens, let's say a 300mm, partly through a bush and let the autumn leaves cascade in front of the lens while you focus on a friend who is standing 15 metres beyond, you can make a picture in which she is in sharp focus, but surrounded by gentle swirls of colour. The shallowest depth of field will make the leaves blurred and soft.

You may spot late afternoon shadows from a row of trees falling across a country road. Because a long lens covers a narrow field of view, you can isolate the shadows. And since the lens also compresses distance, the shadows will appear "stacked up," one behind the other. When a cyclist appears in the distance, you could capture him as he passes momentarily between two shadows and into the sunlight, providing a striking contrast to the linear composition and establishing a definite centre of interest. The photograph on page 150 shows the effect of using a telephoto lens for this kind of image.

You may wish to consider buying a *zoom lens* or lenses. The advantages of a zoom are easy to see. First, you are buying not merely one lens, but a series of lenses wrapped up in a single package. A zoom lens enables you to make compositions impossible to achieve even with a choice of four or five different lenses, because a zoom allows for the most minute adjustments over its entire range. Also, the price is right. A zoom lens may cost more than a fixed-focal-length lens but what you gain in versatility is worth the extra cost. And it's a lot easier to carry around one or two lenses than several. For example, a 28 - 85mm and a 70 - 210mm zoom lens will provide a range of focal lengths adequate for most photographers' needs most of the time. Even if you already own a long lens consider buying an 80 - 200mm zoom. This range of focal lengths will be more useful to you than a longer zoom, such as 300 – 600mm, unless your needs are highly specialized.

Another way to obtain telephoto capability is to use a *tele extender*, an optical device that doubles or triples the focal length of a lens. With tele extenders the minimum focusing distance of the original lens remains unchanged, which is important. However, less light reaches the film, and images may be distorted, a disadvantage that is not too evident at small lens openings. A good tele extender combined with a good lens can make a useful combination; but a tele extender will magnify optical faults as well as the image size, so a good tele extender with a poor lens can be a bad combination. A tele extender is worth considering because it is cheaper than a new telephoto lens and is easier to carry.

The *standard lens* is important too. Don't overlook it. Because it records perspective very much as the human eye sees it, the standard lens is especially useful for documentation. The photographs on pages 94 and 132 were made with a standard lens. If you are serious about exploring the capabilities of your equipment, there is no better exercise than to start with a standard lens and to use it for months, even years, before you buy additional lenses.

Lens speed. There is another characteristic besides focal length by which lenses are classified. This is speed. The speed of a lens is determined by its largest aperture. The smaller the number of a len's widest opening or f/stop, the *faster* the lens. For example, a lens with a maximum aperture of f/1.2 is faster than one of f/1.8.

The speed of a lens affects two aspects of photographic control – exposure and depth of field. The faster a lens is, the shorter the duration of exposure can be. For instance, if you have two 100mm lenses, one with a maximum aperture of f/4 and the other with a maximum aperture of f/2.8, you may have to shoot at $\frac{1}{30}$ second at f/4 with the first lens in order to expose properly, but under the same light conditions you can use the second lens at $\frac{1}{60}$ second at f/2.8 – half the exposure time. However, the faster lens will give you less depth of field at its maximum aperture than the slower lens.

Most manufacturers offer more than one speed of lens for a given focal length. There are often two 300mm lenses available for a particular camera, for example. Given a choice between a 300mm f/5.6 lens and a 300mm f/4 lens, consider buying the slower lens for three reasons. The first and most obvious reason is price. The slower lens will probably be quite a bit less expensive than the faster one. The second reason is size and weight. The faster lens is likely to be bigger and heavier. This means that if you are hand holding your camera at a sports event, you'll have to use a higher shutter speed with the faster lens – in order to overcome camera movement – than you will with the slower one. You may be able to hand hold the f/5.6 lens at $\frac{1}{125}$ second, if you are very steady, but you'll almost certainly have to shoot at $\frac{1}{250}$ second to assure sharpness with the heavier f/4 lens. This means that you lose any exposure advantage immediately. The third reason is optical quality. Many slow lenses have a long history of development and use so that most aberrations have long since been removed.

Putting your camera on a tripod still won't give you an edge with the faster lens. For example, if you are using an aperture of f/11, you'll need the same shutter speed for both lenses to get equivalent exposures. If you are using maximum apertures on both lenses, you will require one shutter speed slower for the f/5.6 lens than for the f/4, but since your camera is held steady on a tripod the slower speed won't make much difference to you in most circumstances. In short, don't buy fast telephoto lenses unless you have personal reasons for doing so, reasons which have emerged clearly from the specific technical demands of your photography.

The same advice is relevant for standard and wide-angle lenses. Many photographers never require fast lenses such as f/1.2 and f/1.4. An f/2.8 lens is more than adequate for nearly every conceivable exposure situation, and allows you to achieve extremely shallow depth of field whenever you want it. So, when you have a choice, consider buying a slower lens, rather than a faster one, and take the money you save to buy yourself a new supply of film.

Tripods

There are two important reasons for using a tripod. It steadies the camera. And it induces visual and technical discipline. Either reason is sufficient cause for buying and using a tripod. Together, they are compelling causes – especially for the beginner.

It's quite true that there are some kinds of photography for which a tripod is always a hindrance, such as candid photography of people and certain sports, and if you specialize in one of these areas you won't use a tripod very often. It's also true that every photographer from time to time encounters situations where a tripod is a great bother. But for most photographers most of the time, there is much to be gained by standing your camera on three legs. Cameras, like people, function best when they are well supported.

Take steadiness. Careful tests have proven that hand-held pictures taken at $\frac{1}{60}$ second on a 35mm camera just aren't as sharp as pictures made with a tripod-supported camera. You don't have to blow up your negatives or transparencies very far in order to see the difference – even if you're as steady as the Rock of Gibraltar and often attempt shooting at speeds as slow as $\frac{1}{8}$ second.

Take discipline. The very act of placing the tripod in position induces care in making the photograph. You compose a photograph in the same way as when you are hand holding; if you don't like your camera position, you can easily reposition your tripod until you find the viewpoint you want. But because the tripod and not the photographer is holding the camera, you don't get tired keeping that position. Fewer kinks in the elbows!

You'll find it easier to consider the design of each image and make fine adjustments when you are using a tripod. You'll be able to study the effect of lines more carefully, and note more accurately the proportion of the main subject in relation to the entire picture space. And, if light is fairly constant, you can study the intensity of light in different areas and note the tonal relationships between these areas. If you buy a tripod when you begin making photographs and use it constantly, you will help to educate yourself visually and you will be forever grateful for the wisdom of your decision.

Here are some important factors to consider when you select a tripod.

1 / A tripod should be sturdy, unlikely to tremble in a strong wind or to fall over under the weight of your heaviest camera or longest lens. You do not need a big or heavy tripod unless your camera is large and you have some very long or very heavy lenses.

2 / A tripod for 35mm or slightly larger-format cameras should *not* have a pan head, which is invariably what is fitted on top. This pan head is for movie or video cameras, not still cameras, and why virtually all tripods are manufactured and sold with them is a complete and enduring mystery to me. Frankly, the pan head is a curse. Before you leave the camera store with your new tripod make sure that you can unscrew the pan head. Give it back to the clerk and buy a ball-and-socket head in its place.

A ball-and-socket head allows you to swivel your camera on the tripod and to tilt it in any direction. It enables you to make very minute adjustments in composition, so you'll find it easier to get precisely the design you want. These things are much more difficult to do with most pan heads, and besides, a pan head has a handle which often sticks out where you don't want it. The ball-and-socket head has a knob (or two) which replaces the handle, allows for greater and easier manoeuvrability, and doesn't get in your way.

A Leitz ball-and-socket head has great durability and strength. It is virtually indestructible, exceedingly versatile, simple to use, easily holds lenses up to 300mm and even longer, and will make working with your tripod a real joy. The Leitz head may seem costly, but it is worth every cent of the price. There are also other good brands.

3 / At the tripod's minimum height you should be able to spread the legs wide enough to permit the use of close-up equipment for subjects on the ground.

4 / The legs should have adjustable rubber tips which will screw down to protect floors and carpets.

5 / Examine the construction of your tripod to see how the legs are attached. Watch out for tripods which have screws or nuts on the inside of the legs near the top. If these screws come loose, it may be nearly impossible to tighten them because of their position. Also avoid rivets in hinged joints as they cannot be tightened.

6 / A tripod for 35mm cameras does not need leg braces attached to the centre post, unless you often use very long lenses and require the extra stability.

7 / A tripod which has clips or twist knobs for extending or shortening the legs is

usually easier to operate than one with rings.

8 / A tripod should have a centre post which is easy to remove, preferably one which does not have gears and a crank. Sometimes you may want to place your camera upside down between the legs in order to get a better composition. The removable post permits this, as well as the insertion of a very short centre post (which you can usually buy with the tripod as an extra). A short post can be very useful when you are working close to the ground.

9 / A small, fully collapsible tripod is very useful for long hikes, sports events, and travel by air. A good size for most suitcases is one which does not exceed 56 centimetres in length and 9 centimetres in diameter, and weighs 2 kilograms or a little less.

10 / Buy a couple of cable releases when you get your tripod. A cable release allows you to trip the shutter without touching the camera, and thus assures that the tripod will not shake during the exposure. A locking cable release is useful for long time exposures.

Finally, I'd like to pass on a suggestion about using your tripod. Once you've completed your composition, stand back before you press the cable release. Don't hang on to the tripod. Don't keep peeking through the viewfinder, unless you're watching a moving object. And don't bounce up and down on the surrounding earth. Stand up, stand back, and stand still, and make your photograph with the confidence that you've done everything you possibly can.

Flash

An electronic flash unit may be extremely useful, depending on the kind of photography you do. If you are a parent with small children around the house, a flash can be a worthwhile investment. If your interest is primarily landscapes and holiday scenes, think twice before you buy. (For discussion of flash and how to use it, see "Using flash," pages 114 to 117.)

Filters

You'll need filters much more frequently for black-and-white photography than for colour. A great many colour photographers rarely use filters. In any case, if you're buying filters, you'll need one set for black-and-white and another set for colour.

Filters for black-and-white photography. Black-and-white films reproduce all colours as tones of grey. A bright red object may turn out to be almost the same tone of grey as a rich green one, on black-and-white film. The two objects will lack the contrast which colour provided. In order to ensure that you have contrast between the two, use a filter to make the red and green appear as different tones. A green filter will block much of the red reflected from the red object, but will allow the green light from the green object to reach the film. Thus, the red object will be underexposed or darker than the green one, and contrast will be achieved. A red filter will perform in the reverse manner, making the red object a much lighter tone of grey than the green object, but you will still have contrast. A yellow filter will darken a blue sky, and a red filter will darken it even more, making clouds stand out dramatically.

Pick up a manual on filters for black-and-white films at your camera store, and study it before you buy your filters. When you purchase a set of filters, don't wait until you need them before you use them. Experiment with them right away, so you can see the results. Then when you do need a filter, you'll know which one to choose.

Most filters require some exposure correction. The filter manual, or the instruction sheet, will tell you what aperture or time adjustment is needed. It is not always wise to assume that the camera light meter will give the correct exposure, as some types of meters may be more or less sensitive to certain colours. Experiment and mark the filter rim with any correction that is needed.

Filters for colour photography. Filters for colour films shift all the colours in a photograph toward the colour of the filters. A blue filter makes everything bluish; a yellow filter makes everything golden. Usually filters for colour films are used to "correct" inappropriate colour. For example, tungsten lights cast a very "warm" glow. If you use daylight film to photograph a person who is illuminated by a light bulb, her skin will appear red. If you add a blue filter to the front of your lens, your subject will have more normal skin colour, because the blue will balance the colour of the warm light.

However, if you're not concerned about "true" colour, then you can use a filter to produce any colour effect you want. If you've discovered a stunning pattern of cracks in the sidewalk, but have no intention of photographing it in a realistic manner, you may add a colour filter to enhance the unreality. You can even use a filter designated for black-and-white films and give very bold colour effects. The colours in these filters are much more intense than in filters for colour films.

An ultraviolet or UV filter is useful for colour photography. It eliminates ultraviolet light, thus reducing bluishness and haziness in long distance and aerial shots. Many photographers put one on a lens when they buy it, and never take it off. The colour effect is very slight, and the filter protects the front lens element.

Filters for black-and-white and colour photography. A polarizing filter can be used with both colour and black-and-white films. This filter can be very helpful when bright tones distract from your composition. A polarizing filter does not block all reflected light, but only the light that is polarized – light waves which are oriented at one angle instead of several. You must rotate a polarizing filter on the front of your lens to find the position which will eliminate the amount of polarized light you want removed. Because a polarizing filter blocks out some light, it affects exposure. There are slight variations in different makes of polascreens, but generally they require shooting with the lens opening increased by 1⅓ stops, or by ⅓ stop and one shutter speed slower.

A neutral density filter can also be used for both black-and-white and colour photography. It simply reduces the amount of light reaching the film. This filter is especially useful when you are photographing in bright sun with high-speed film and you need a slower shutter speed to record motion or a larger lens opening to get a shallower depth of field. Neutral density filters are available in various densities, each reducing the exposure by a specific amount.

Close-up equipment
Extension tubes, bellows, close-up lenses, and macro lenses are photographic tools which enable you to focus on objects close to the lens – much closer than the usual minimum focusing distance. If you are interested in nature photography, especially close-ups of flowers or insects, you'll need one or more of these tools.

Extension tubes and *bellows* are devices which you insert between the camera and the lens. You screw or snap the tubes or bellows into the lens mount, and then you put the lens on the other end. Neither tubes nor bellows have any lens elements in them. They merely extend the distance of the lens from the film, which results in your being able to focus on close-up objects. The main difference between the two is that tubes are of fixed lengths, but bellows can be shortened or lengthened and may also have a greater focusing range.

Extension tubes usually come in sets of three, and you can use any one by itself or in combination with the others in order to focus where you want. Tubes are lightweight too, but they have a disadvantage. Since they only give you a shallow focusing range, you must either try different combinations of tubes, or move the camera to the precise spot to get the image you want.

Bellows are somewhat heavier, but have the advantage of being variable in length. You merely turn a knob to shorten or lengthen them – in order to focus on the main subject. Bellows with two tracks are very useful. On one track the bellows is extended or retracted; on the other, the entire camera and bellows can be moved closer to or farther away from your subject matter without moving the tripod. This second track makes working with bellows a pleasure. An alternative to the double-track bellows is a separate single-track or focusing stage which can be used as a second track on your single-track bellows or for fine focusing with other lenses, such as macros.

Although it may seem odd to anybody who does not know much about optics, the shorter the focal length of the lens you use in front of extension tubes or bellows, the larger the image of your subject will be. Conversely, the longer the focal length of the lens, the smaller the image of your subject will be. The ideal range of lenses to use with tubes or bellows is from 50mm to about 135mm. Shorter lenses force you to move so close to the subject that you may bump into it, while longer lenses may be very difficult to support, and actually require a second tripod for support. However, there are exceptions. It's possible to use a 400mm lens in front of a bellows, if the lens and bellows are constructed to work together.

Close-up lenses look like colourless filters, and are like filters in that they screw into the front of a lens. They are also like extension tubes in that they come in sets, usually of three, and may be used singly or in combination with one another. They are fairly simple to use, because you don't have to remove your camera lens in order to change close-up lenses, but you will have to reposition your tripod and camera with each new close-up lens or combination of close-up lenses. Unlike extension tubes or bellows, close-up lenses do not reduce the amount of light reaching the film, and require no exposure adjustment.

The major drawback of these lenses used to be their relatively poor optical quality, which produced pictures that were not very sharp, especially at the edges. The lack of sharpness increased with the number of close-up lenses used together. Nowadays this is less of a problem, since close-up lenses are manufactured to high standards, but it is still a consideration if you expect to make a sizable enlargement from a negative. Extension tubes or bellows, which have no lens elements, do not interfere with the optical quality of the camera lens. Photographers who use colour-slide film and never expect to print their images, but only to project them, probably don't need to worry very much about any loss of sharpness that might occur with close-up lenses, because projector lenses and screens reduce sharpness. So if close-up lenses do cause a lack of sharpness in colour slides, it is unlikely to show in the projected image.

A *macro lens* is probably the best answer to most photographers' needs for close-up work. For practical purposes a macro lens is an ordinary lens (usually 50mm or 100mm) which also focuses on objects much closer to the lens than regular lenses do. With a macro lens, you can shoot a landscape one minute and a bee lighting on a flower the next. It's merely a matter of focusing. A 50mm macro lens is an excellent choice for your first lens, and offers many more picture opportunities than a regular 50mm lens, which usually focuses down to about 45 centimetres. A 50mm macro will focus to about 10 centimetres.

If you already own a 50mm lens, then consider a 100mm macro as a second lens. This will give you a medium telephoto lens with close-up capability. A 100mm macro will focus only about half as close as a 50mm macro, but because a 100mm lens produces twice as big an image as a 50mm lens, you will end up with the same capacity for making close-ups. And, the 100mm macro offers one real advantage – you can stand twice as far from the subject, yet get the same size of image that a 50mm macro would give. This extra distance can be very useful when you are photographing nature subjects, such as insects or grasses covered with dew, because it's easy to frighten some insects or to bump into the grasses and knock off the drops. The photographs on pages 133 and 153 show the types of close-ups you can make with a macro lens.

A macro lens has one drawback, unless you use a bellows or close-up lens with it – it doesn't allow you to magnify your subject. Its maximum capability is a life-size image on a 35mm slide or negative *prior* to projection or enlargement.

A *macro-zoom lens* would appear to be the ideal lens, combining as it does zoom capability plus the capacity for making close-ups. But you don't want a lens that's heavy, awkward to work with, or of dubious optical quality. Also, the close-up capability of most macro-zooms is less than that of ordinary macro lenses. Test before you buy, even if you have to spend an hour zooming and making close-ups right in the camera store. Make sure you try all the f/stops at both the minimum and maximum range of the zoom and in the macro position. If the resulting pictures are sharp at every f/stop and you find the lens easy to work with, then consider a purchase. A macro-zoom makes sense if you have neither a zoom nor a macro at present.

One final note about close-up equipment – you can use various combinations of equipment to get better close-ups or to magnify your subject. For example, it's possible to use extension tubes behind your camera lens with the close-up lenses in front of it. Or, you can use extension tubes and bellows together. It's a good idea to try out various combinations and to make some notes on how well they work. How much enlargement do you get? Is the combination of equipment easy or difficult to work with? If you are familiar with the possibilities, you will be able to choose the right combination of equipment when you need it.

Assessing your needs
Buy only the equipment which will help you make the pictures you want. For instance, if you use your camera extensively on trips and holidays, and want versa-

tility without carrying too many items or too much weight, consider the following combinations of equipment: 1/a 24 or 28mm wide-angle lens, a standard 50mm lens, an 80 - 200mm zoom lens, and a set of extension tubes; 2/a 28 - 85mm zoom, an 80 - 200mm zoom, and one of extension tubes, close-up lenses, or a macro lens; 3/ a 28 - 85mm zoom and an 80 - 200mm zoom, one of which has macro capability. Many photographers will have at least one of the above items, and will need to add only one more item to complete a set.

If you photograph mainly people in your home or neighbourhood, or are primarily interested in arranging and photographing still lifes, draw up similar brief lists of equipment which will meet most of your needs. It's a quick way to identify the equipment you still need.

Remember that photographs, not equipment, are what photography is all about. Seeing and making pictures is the real challenge. The simplest equipment can be sufficient to give you years of enjoyment, as long as you keep exploring its potential. So, when you buy something new, make sure that you are investing not only in equipment, but also in new visual experiences.

Caring for your equipment

Virtually all cameras and lenses are so well constructed that the amateur need never worry about wearing them out or damaging them, short of a major accident. This does not mean that every part will always function perfectly. The shutter may jam, the self-timer may stop working, or the meter may go on the blink, but it is rare indeed to find a camera that has succumbed to old age.

Perhaps the most common fear is what will happen when a camera gets wet. The answer is, probably nothing. Don't stay inside just because it's raining. Go out, but be sensible. Keep your camera inside your coat or camera bag until you are ready to use it. If it's raining very hard, cover it with a small sheet of plastic when setting it up. One photographer I know has, on her tripod, a clamp which will hold an umbrella handle. The umbrella keeps both the camera and the photographer dry. I wear a big black stetson over the hood of my raincoat on a wet day; when I want to leave my camera sitting on the tripod for any reason, I place the stetson over my camera and walk away. (This has been known to hold up traffic. A black stetson with three metal legs is not something you see by the roadside every day – even in Alberta.)

If your camera gets very wet, wipe it off gently when you come inside. Dry the lens with a very soft chamois or lens tissue. If you suspect that water has leaked inside, remove the lens and dry out the interior of the camera with the gentle flow of warm air from a hair dryer. You can do the same thing with the back of the camera, after you've rewound your film of course. The hair dryer is a very useful tool, particularly in an emergency. A couple of photographers I know have used it to dry out a camera which they dropped into a brook – and apparently with complete success; but they were lucky!

If you drop your camera into salt water, however, you are in trouble. The best advice I can give is "Don't do it!" – especially if it is not insured. Salt corrosion is the biggest danger; so, as soon as possible (preferably before the camera dries at all), submerge it in fresh water and rinse, rinse, rinse. Then prepare to spend an afternoon with the hair dryer. This may salvage the camera, but it is less likely to help the lens. Don't hold your breath – in either case. The chances for rehabilitation are not good, especially with electronic cameras.

Perhaps the greatest threat to the average camera and lens is getting dirt or sand into moving parts. If you do, don't muck about! Get the equipment cleaned professionally. Don't worry about a little dust on the lens, because it won't affect optical quality. Get rid of it when you must with a small air blower (available at any camera store), and remove anything sticky with a tiny drop of lens cleaner absorbed in lens tissue or a very soft chamois. Some very careful photographers don't use liquid cleaner at all, but simply breathe (*not* blow) on the lens and then wipe it with the chamois or lens tissue. Before you use a chamois for this purpose, it should have been washed a few times to remove stiffness. Use a real chamois, not an imitation.

The way to care for your equipment is simply to use common sense. 1/Keep your camera clean inside and out by careful wiping, or by brushing with a camel-hair brush, or by blowing air from a small air blower. Both brush and blower are available from your camera dealer. Sometimes they are manufactured and sold as a single unit. If dirt or dust accumulates on the reflex mirror, use only a blower to remove it. 2/Keep the cap on the lens when you aren't making pictures, and also make sure a cap is on the rear of the lens when the lens is off the camera. 3/Shut off the light meter when you aren't using it, to protect the life of the battery. 4/Buy a small jeweller's screwdriver, and periodically check all the tiny screws on your camera and lenses, especially after a long plane flight, which may loosen them through vibration. 5/Don't force any moving parts which seem to be stuck or locked, especially in cold weather. 6/Remove the camera from its case when you put it on a tripod; it may be nearly impossible to remove both camera and case later on. 7/Pack your equipment carefully for travelling, taking special care to ensure that no lenses or cameras will bounce or rub against each other. 8/Don't leave your camera lying around or standing on a tripod where children are playing. 9/Never leave a camera or tripod unattended in a high wind. 10/Don't store

your equipment or film where it will be subjected to high temperatures or humidity, especially for a long period. If possible, store your film at below 12°C.
11/Have your camera professionally cleaned and checked every couple of years, or more often if you have been using it frequently.

Because cameras are so well constructed, a photographer does not have to treat them with kid gloves. Cameras are made to be used, not admired. If you badly want a photograph which involves some risk to your equipment, take the risk. Cameras are replaceable; opportunities are not.

Films

Some photographers seem to think that selecting film is like choosing a husband or wife. In fact, some photographers seem far more committed to a particular film than they are to their spouse. However, no film is perfect. All colour and all black-and-white films have certain characteristics which make them excellent choices for some circumstances, and not so good for others. You can learn a lot about films by reading test reports in popular photographic magazines and trade publications, but you'll never know a film well until you have used it with your own lenses in a variety of situations. No matter how much you read, you can't tell whether you'll like a new model of car until you drive it.

A serious photographer will make fairly regular comparison tests with different films, not just to learn about them initially, but also to develop and retain a feeling about them. There's a very easy way to do this. If, let's say, you're finishing off a roll of Kodachrome 64, leave the camera in position on the tripod as you reload with a roll of Fujichrome. Repeat the last shot on the new roll. You'll only have two photographs for comparison, but the differences may be obvious. If you perform this simple test with various films on a fairly frequent basis, you'll soon have a pretty good collection of comparative material, and you'll find yourself developing a kind of intuitive knowledge of which film is the best choice for the situation in which you're working.

Remember that all manufacturers are continually improving their products, so just because you didn't think much of a particular film two years ago is no reason to ignore it forever. Keep your testing up-to-date. Of course, the quality of a negative or transparency also depends on the quality of the processing, so it certainly helps to do your own developing (provided you're good at it), or to send your test films to a laboratory which maintains strict quality control.

What should you look for in evaluating films? That's a very basic question, but one which I can only answer in part, because every photographer's interests and perceptions differ. All I can do is list objective factors which can be tested. It will be up to you to evaluate the results, according to your personal tastes.

Colour or black-and-white?

First you should consider the most fundamental of all questions about films – which is the better film for your photographic image, colour or black-and-white? While the final answer to this question must be subjective, there is a major objective difference to consider. *The most important element in a black-and-white image is the range of tones or light values, that is, brightness. The most important element in a colour image is colour*, although the range of tones may also be very important.

The implications of this difference are wide-ranging; let me describe a few practical effects. In a black-and-white portrait, the viewer's attention will be drawn to the model's eyes. In a colour portrait, the viewer's attention will often go to the person's lips or clothes. For this reason, consider black-and-white film seriously for making portraits. Colour is frequently unnecessary, and often distracting. But with autumn leaves or sunsets, it's usually colour that catches the photographer's eye, so black-and-white film would be an unlikely choice.

Not all circumstances allow for such an easy decision. In fact, most don't. So, let's consider a less definite situation, such as a winter landscape with just two subjects in it – an expanse of snow and a row of barren trees. Recently I saw two versions of such a scene, one in black and white and one in colour. The decision about which film should be used was made, in each case, on subjective grounds. One of the photographers responds more strongly to forms than to colours, and she knew that black-and-white film would intensify the shapes, lines, and textures by eliminating any attention that might be paid to colour, even though the colour saturation was very weak.

The other photographer chose colour because his main emotional response was to the colour. He was struck by the starkness of the trees against the snow, but the warm colour of early twilight softened the harshness for him. He decided to record the bleakness and the gentleness in one image – to show that the contrast of impressions produced its own harmony. Both photographers were successful in expressing their emotional response to this winter landscape.

Choosing between colour or black-and-white film seems to be a natural process for most photographers. But you should try to analyse your choice and also familiarize yourself with the different characteristics of the films.

Characteristics of films

Let's look at the objective characteristics by which films can be evaluated, and what these may mean to your photography.

Brilliance is an important consideration when you select colour films. Extensive comparison tests I have conducted with two Kodak colour films proved that, on my equipment, one brand of film always rendered hues more brilliantly than the other. Since I usually prefer muted colours, I will avoid using this film except when the colours in my subject are, to begin with, somewhat more muted than I want. But, if I want to be certain of a strong, dramatic rendition of hues, I'll choose the film which regularly produces it.

When it comes to *colour* itself, opinions may differ. Not everybody agrees on what is normal or natural colour. Human response to colour is conditioned by both physical and psychological factors. You are the only one who can determine which films will render the various hues more accurately for you in different situations.

Speed is the measure of a film's sensitivity to light. Some films respond to light more quickly than others. A film with a low sensitivity to light is known as a "slow" film, one with high sensitivity is known as a "fast" film. The speed of a film is indicated (both on the cardboard box and on the film cassette itself) in the form of an exposure index or ISO rating. Films with ISO ratings of 25 or less are slow; from 50 to about 125 are medium; and from 160 to 320 are fast. Any ISO rating above 400 indicates a very fast film by present standards.

You should choose a high-speed film when you want to freeze action, such as a runner crossing the finish line, or when you want to photograph in low light, but don't have a tripod with you. Choose a slow film when you want to be sure of making long exposures. For instance, it's much easier to give a sense of movement in water, or blur in wind-tossed flowers, if you can shoot at $\frac{1}{8}$ second instead of at $\frac{1}{125}$ second under a given intensity of light.

The colours rendered by a film should be the same for all exposure times and light intensities. This is the law of reciprocity. But if exposure times are either very long or very short, or if light intensities are very high or very low, the law of reciprocity fails. Different films react in different ways to reciprocity failure. The colour balance of a film changes and the resulting image may have an overall colour cast.

The effect of changes in shutter speeds on the way films reproduce colours is barely noticeable between the middle speeds of $\frac{1}{250}$ to $\frac{1}{30}$ second, may be slightly noticeable between $\frac{1}{500}$ or $\frac{1}{15}$ to $\frac{1}{8}$ second, and can be easy to see after that. The effect is sometimes pronounced with time exposures.

If you want to change the colours in your picture, choose a slow film for a dark situation, so you'll be forced into long exposures. I'm speaking here of exposures of one second to a minute or more. For example, it's my experience (given the films' characteristics as I write this) that Ektachrome daylight films will become "warmer" the longer they are exposed, but that Kodachrome 25 will not. So, if I'm in dark woods photographing a white mushroom surrounded by green moss, I may choose Ektachrome to avoid the accentuated greens and blues which the Kodachrome could produce. If I'm photographing a white mushroom surrounded by brown leaves, I may choose Kodachrome 25 over Ektachrome because, in long exposures, my experience indicates that Ektachromes will respond positively to browns and make them appear more reddish. Fujichrome will do the same thing. Kodachrome 25, on the other hand, does not tend to be red in a long exposure. It must be emphasized, however, that the characteristics of films are continually being tested by the manufacturers and improvements are being made regularly. It's quite possible that the responses of the films mentioned here will be changed. The important thing is to remember that colour shifts do occur, and to make your own tests with current film stock.

High-speed colour films, which tend to give somewhat less colour brilliance at any time, lose both brilliance and contrast more swiftly in long exposures than slower-speed films. So, if you want to mute existing colours, choose a high-speed Ektachrome, for example, and make the longest exposure you can.

Gradation is the term used to describe a film's ability to reproduce contrast or a range of dark, light, and intermediate tones. (This subject is also discussed in "Properties of light," pages 52 to 54, and "Directions of light," pages 55 to 60.) It's an important measure for both black-and-white and colour films, but especially the former.

In high-contrast film the transition between different tones tends to be abrupt. In other words, there is a strong tendency to lights and darks, and a de-emphasis of middle tones. A low-contrast film performs in the opposite way, emphasizing the middle tones, and softening the lightest and darkest areas. A medium-contrast film produces negatives or transparencies with no emphasis on any particular part of the range of tones; it will give good solid dark and light tones and a wide range of intermediate tones. Consequently, medium-contrast films are the most useful films for most photographers most of the time. A film's ability to reproduce contrast is related to its speed. Slow-speed films generally produce the greatest contrast, and high-speed films the least. Any black-and-white film will produce more contrast if the negative is underexposed and overdeveloped, and less contrast if it is overexposed and underdeveloped.

The *latitude* of a film is its ability to tolerate overexposure and underexposure and still produce an acceptable image. Most films are very tolerant of overexposure and underexposure, but colour films have less latitude than black-and-white ones. They still produce acceptable exposures (depending on the subject matter and lighting) when underexposed up to three stops, or when overexposed up to two stops. But this is a subjective evaluation, and you may want to stretch the limits under certain conditions. Latitude is also related to film speed. In general, slow-speed films have more latitude than fast ones.

Films have a granular structure or *graininess*. This is caused by the irregular distribution and overlapping of silver-bromide crystals, which reproduce grey tones as tiny, separate dots. The larger the crystals, the more graininess will be apparent. Fast films have larger crystals than slow films.

The visual effects of grain are very important to consider when selecting black-and-white films. To begin with, all black-and-white negatives, potentially, will end up as prints, and not much enlargement is required before the grain structure of a film starts to show. Select a high-speed film if you want a lot of grain, and intensify it through overexposure and overdevelopment. If you don't want grain, select a very slow-speed film, and develop the film normally.

Grain is of little importance to the average amateur who shoots colour slides, because projector lenses and screen surfaces reduce the appearance of grain. In normal projection of slides, nobody will ever notice it. However, the presence or absence of grain is of much greater importance to photographers who want fine enlargements from colour slides or colour negatives.

All films have certain objective characteristics to which the photographer will respond subjectively. This is why it's essential to depend less on manufacturers' reports and other photographers' evaluations, and more on your own tests made with your own equipment. See for yourself, feel for yourself, and judge for yourself. In choosing film, as in practically every other facet of photography, you should not deny yourself the pleasure of discovery and the satisfaction of personal experience.

Learning to see

Discipline

The first year that I made photographs seriously I used a tripod for every picture –
no matter what the situation, and whether I really needed one or not. The use of a
tripod induces care. Good photographers are careful people. They're disciplined.
In that first year I learned how essential discipline is. I learned that fine images
don't happen – they are made! And made very, very carefully.

I still use a tripod for making most of my photographs, but even when I don't, I
think as if I were. I react in the same way. It's second nature now. Once you've
learned how, you never forget. But this is not about tripods; I've talked about them
already. Rather, it's about being thoughtful and deliberate, about taking time to
consider all the details which will affect your final exposure.

Let me give you an example. Behind my house there's a small meadow which
changes dramatically with the seasons. If I go out on a dew-drenched summer
morning to watch the first rays of sunlight streaming through the daisies and the
wild roses, I will probably become euphoric. And, if I decide to photograph the
meadow, I will make certain that my subjective response plays a fundamental part
in how I go about making pictures. In fact, it's really both the scene and my
subjective response that I'll want to capture.

So, chances are that one thing I will do is carefully consider deliberate use of
overexposure to lighten colours and to intensify the whites of the rising mists and
the silver of the sun's rays. I want to record and to convey lightness, delicacy, and
gentleness, not only because the scene shows me these things, but also because I
feel them. In fact, many people respond to light tones and gentle colours with
feelings of delicacy and ease, and often with a sense of exhilaration.

If I go into the same field in the slanting sunlight of a November afternoon,
when the brown grasses are etched upon the meadow in a sort of military progression, when they are stiffened into a rigidity that no super-starch could ever

produce, my response and my instructions to the camera will be quite different.

Gone is my euphoria. Gone is my exhilaration. Now my fascination is with symmetry and shape, with line and form. As I look at the individual stalks of grass, I notice that every one is illuminated brightly on the south and darkened by shadow on the north. So, I stand to the east or west in order to see both light and dark, and choose an exposure which will retain the highlights but let the shadows go very black. I want the sharp tonal distinctions. I need the contrast. To get this, I will give slightly less exposure than what the meter indicates is the "correct" reading. The choice is mine, and I make it on the basis of how the subject matter appears to me, and how I feel about it.

Fine images depend upon thinking about what you see and understanding what you feel about what you see. Fine images demand careful preparation. The more careful you are when you begin photography, the easier you'll find it later on. There are no shortcuts. And there is no greater pleasure in photography than achieving the image you set out to capture or create.

Properties of light

Light has three characteristics which photographers must understand. These are brightness, quality, and colour. They have a major bearing on how and what people see and feel. Sudden differences in brightness or quality of light, and changes in colour, can rapidly alter a person's mood. All three characteristics have strong symbolic value as well.

Being aware of the human response to these characteristics of light is just as important to a photographer as knowing the amount of light required to make an exposure on film. In some respects it's more important, because it's easier to calculate the quantity of light needed for a good exposure than it is to understand why people respond to light as they do. The control of light is fundamental to all photography, whether black-and-white or colour. Let's consider the three characteristics of light in turn.

Brightness is the measure of the intensity of light. A pure black object reflects no light at all. A pure white object reflects all the light which strikes it. Between the two lies a continuum of grey tones – from almost pure black to almost pure white. This continuum or range of tones is subject to constant scrutiny by photographers who work with black-and-white films. Unfortunately, colour photographers often pay it too little attention, even though it is important in making satisfactory colour images.

All photographers must consider carefully the various tones within the picture area. They must decide the amount of light tones they want in comparison to the amount of middle or dark tones. They must be aware of small isolated areas of a particular tone which will become accent points.

One of the best exercises for a beginning photographer is to study a scene or object, and translate all colours into shades of light and dark – to see the picture entirely in terms of its areas of brightness. Objects are not merely red or green or blue. They are also light and dark and in between in infinite gradations. Effective visual statement depends on the photographer's ability to recognize these distinctions, because if the photographer does not recognize them, he cannot control them.

Colour photographers should be aware of two basic facts about tonal range. 1/If an image has a limited range of colours, it must have an extended range of tones, or contrast of tones, for composition to occur. 2/If an image has a limited range of tones, it must have an extended range of colours, or contrast of colours, for composition to occur. In other words, design is impossible in an image which is restricted to one colour and one tone.

These basic facts are illustrated by the photographs on pages 22, 23, and 18. 1 / The colours and tones of the first two photographs are almost identical. In both cases the brightest area becomes the centre of interest. However, because of the lighting, the river of reflected trees is the strongest visual element in the picture on page 22, whereas in the other the reflections are a backdrop for the bright green grass. The subject matter reverses roles. The grass and reflections in the picture on page 23 form a one-colour or monochromatic image as in the preceding picture. Therefore, the contrast of tones is important to both compositions. 2 / The photograph on page 18 is extremely unusual in one respect – it contains almost no variation in tone. When tonal variety is absent, there must be a colour difference if composition is to occur. Therefore the spot of yellow is fundamental. As a black-and-white print the image would virtually disappear, becoming little more than a grey card. The converse of this picture, then, is a black-and-white print containing only two tones, because it's equally true that, when colour variety is missing, there must be a difference of tones, if composition is to occur.

The **quality** of light has to do with its harshness or softness. Direct or harsh light emanates from a point-like source, like the sun or a light bulb, and tends to accentuate tonal differences or contrasts. Soft or indirect light occurs when the source of illumination is obscured and light is diffused before it reflects off the subject. Cloudy days give soft light, because the clouds prevent sunlight from reaching us directly. Clouds diffuse light, as does a canopy of leaves, or a flash which is "bounced" off a ceiling rather than being aimed directly at the subject. The quality of light has a strong bearing on the mood of a picture.

Under harsh light tonal differences are abrupt, and contrasts appear stronger. Under soft light, tonal differences are seldom abrupt, and brightness shades gradually from light to dark. Contrast is less definite, although usually the extremes of brightness are still there, at least to the trained eye. Under soft light the intermediate tones are increased and play a greater role in composition.

The third important characteristic of light is ***colour***. The colour of daylight varies enormously between dawn and dusk. In most cases photographers accept these variations and appreciate them. Who, for example, would want to filter the gold out of a sunset? Of course, different kinds of artificial illumination affect the way films reproduce colour, and photographers quite often use certain films or filters which correct the colour for "normal" perception by the human eye.

The basic problem facing a photographer is not to obtain accurate colour, but rather to produce colour which is appropriate to the subject or to his feeling about it. For example, if a person's face appears slightly green, because he is standing in the reflected light of a green building, the photographer will want to correct it. On the other hand, a blue cast on ice and snow adds to the feeling of chill, and is probably acceptable.

Photographers should try to make use of the symbolic values and psychological effects of the three properties of light – brightness, quality, and colour. There's no doubt that a bright day affects us differently from a dark day. Similarly, we feel differently at twilight than we do at dawn, and it's not just because we've worked all day. The presence or absence of light, or more accurately, the presence or absence of tones within a picture, and the relative amounts of those tones which are present all play important roles in our emotional response.

Photographers must constantly assess both the light they need for exposing film and the effect which that light will have on viewers of the completed image.

Directions of light

Each angle of lighting creates specific visual effects or opportunities, and each causes special problems. One of the great pleasures of making pictures, or of just using your eyes well at any time, is in observing the direction in which light falls and the effect this has on the subject.

Direct lighting

There are, basically, three directions from which direct light can fall on your subject: on the front, on the side (one side or other), or on the back. These directions of light are called, simply, front lighting, side lighting, and back lighting. Each direction tends to produce certain visual and emotional effects, so each has advantages and disadvantages. Before you think about exposure, you must recognize the direction of the light you're dealing with.

Front lighting occurs when the sun is behind you and the light from it is falling directly on the subject in front of your camera, as in the photograph on page 64. This is the kind of lighting beginners in photography feel most comfortable with, usually as a result of being told, "Make sure the sun is over your shoulder!" It's also the kind of lighting you get when you point a flash gun directly at your subject.

Front lighting can produce dramatic results, especially if the main subject is lighter than its surroundings – like a clump of birches standing at the edge of an evergreen forest. The sun streaming down on the forest is reflected back strongly from the birches, but not from the spruces and hemlocks. So the clump of birches stands out from the rest of the trees. In a situation like this, the effect of front lighting commands your attention. It's the reason for your picture. If the sun had not been shining or had been shining from any other direction, you might not have noticed the birches at all.

However, front lighting is often the least interesting form of lighting, simply because the shadows which your subject casts fall behind it. This means that the lines and dark tones of the shadows are eliminated from your composition, so it will have less visual variety. If you have no shadows, then you must make sure that the space surrounding your centre of interest is well used in other ways.

Side lighting occurs when your light source is to one side or other of the picture area and the shadows are falling across it, as in the photograph on page 66. (Light streaming in from a corner is usually referred to as side lighting as well, although technically it's halfway between side lighting and back lighting, or side lighting and front lighting.) Side lighting is exciting because 1/the shadows contain deep tones which contrast with the highlights of the image; 2/the shadows appear as lines of varying thickness and become important visual elements in their own right; 3/these shadows give the impression of a third dimension; and 4/textures tend to be emphasized. A photographer should capitalize on these assets.

Some of the most pleasant side lighting occurs early or late in the day when shadows are long and the light itself is warm. The direction and length of shadows and the colour of light at these times of day tend to produce a richness of colour and tones which is difficult to explain, but easy to see. People like it, and photographers tend to become more active as afternoon wears on toward evening.

One problem with side lighting is an excess of exciting tones, lines, and forms. There's almost too much on the plate. So, be selective. You will have to sort out the elements with your eye, and unless you're looking for a richly tapestried effect, start to eliminate things which will simply clutter your picture. Whether you're photographing a city street, a sweeping mountain landscape, or a few square centimetres of a meadow, the problem is the same. Suggest more by saying less. Six or seven strong bars caused by alternating lines of sun and shadow will probably be more effective than fifty – most of the time. You can make successful pictures which contain a lot of shadows, but you should be careful in each case to include little else, so the design is not destroyed.

Back lighting occurs when you are facing the sun, as in the photographs on pages 68 and 131. The light is now falling on the back of your subject, and produces silhouettes and halos. It's strong and dramatic, because it usually causes abrupt and extreme tonal changes. Where whites stop, blacks often begin with little or no intermediate tone.

Back lighting makes real demands on a photographer. Good composition is often far from easy, and the best exposure may be difficult to determine and even harder to achieve. But don't let these minor annoyances stop you. Treat back lighting the same way you must treat every photographic situation. Use its advantages. Play on its strengths!

What are these advantages? 1/The sharp delineation of forms; 2/the creation of bold light and dark tones, with a reduction of detail in shadow areas; and 3/a greater sense of depth, because shadows are falling from the background toward the foreground. Back lighting simplifies and strengthens design and helps to produce strong graphic images.

Back lighting creates a heightened sense of the visually dramatic, and this in turn produces strong human emotional response. Anybody putting a slide show together should consider placing excellent back-lighted photographs at critical points in the sequence, especially after a series of softer, more gentle images. But do it sparingly. A little well-spaced drama is better than a constant diet.

There are problems in using back lighting to compose photographs. Sometimes you get too much black throughout the picture space, or too much black in one area, or annoying things such as straight black lines (tree trunks, perhaps) rising out of unrelated forms (a rather round boulder, for example). In order to avoid these graphic conflicts, or at least to reduce them as much as possible, you will have to position your camera with care. That may be difficult to do if the sun is streaming into your lens. If it is, stop your lens down to f/16 or f/22 and press the depth-of-field preview button to darken the image and make viewing easier.

Don't worry about pointing your lens directly at the sun. With today's single-lens reflex cameras nothing will happen to the camera or its shutter, or lens. However, be careful of your eyes. Stop the lens down to f/16 or f/22, press the depth-of-field preview button, and don't gaze too long into the sun when making your composition.

A common question about back lighting is "How do I get rid of lens flare?" Sometimes, by carefully tilting the camera up or down, or to the left or right, lens flare will disappear. Your composition will be altered, but probably not so severely that you will have to abandon it. Also, by using a lens hood, you may be able to eliminate flare without altering your composition. You can, of course, learn to live with lens flare. If you start to think of it as an asset, you're playing a whole new ball game with the sun.

Back-lighted situations can produce difficulties in determining exposure. The whole topic of exposure comes later, but it's necessary to talk about it here.

There's a rule of thumb that says, in back-lighted situations you follow what your meter tells you and then open up one f/stop. If you're getting a reading of $\frac{1}{250}$ second at f/16, try $\frac{1}{250}$ second at f/11 instead, or use $\frac{1}{125}$ second at f/16 if you don't want to lose any depth of field. This formula assumes that every photographer wants some detail in the shadow areas of every back-lighted composition he makes.

Of course, there are exceptions. At sunset, for instance, you should consider closing down half an f/stop from the meter reading in order to retain the richness of colours in the sky. If the meter says $\frac{1}{60}$ second at f/8, you will go to $\frac{1}{60}$ second between f/8 and f/11. So what it comes down to is that you, the photographer, have to make up your own mind about what you want your final image to look like.

Before you even put your camera on your tripod you may want to approach your subject and take some sample light readings. What does your meter say about the dark side of the big rock? What is it telling you when you point it at the grass? What is the exposure of the sky when the sun is slightly obscured by the branches of a tree? And so on. What you're looking for is a *range* of light values or tones, particularly the values of the most important elements in your composition. Make a mental note of them, then go back to your camera, compose your picture, and determine the depth of field you want. After these things are done, you can choose the overall exposure you want. It's always the last thing you should do before you trip the shutter release.

How do you choose? If the sun is unclouded, bright, fairly high in the sky and shining directly into the lens, $\frac{1}{250}$ second or $\frac{1}{500}$ second at f/16 will work every time with a film of ISO 50 or 64. You'll choose the slower shutter speed if you want a slightly lighter blue in the sky and a little more detail in the landforms. You'll choose the faster speed if you want to produce bold colours and tones and a strong sense of the dramatic. In either case it's doubtful that your picture will be successful if all the bright is in the sky and all the dark is in the land. Try to be observant and thoughtful enough to include secondary highlights in the dark areas in order to give balance to your composition – ripples of light on water, a halo of white fuzz around a leaf, or an icy roadway in the foreground. With many lenses, shooting directly at the sun will also give a star effect, if the lens is set at the smallest aperture.

Most back-lighted compositions do not include the light source, but they do have strong highlights in them and strong blacks as well. The whites can only get so white, as you admit more light through the lens. There is nothing whiter than white; so as you open up your lens you are not making the whites whiter. You are making the greys lighter and turning black into greys. That may be desirable – or not.

Conversely, there is nothing blacker than black. So when you progressively reduce the amount of light reaching the film, you are making the highlights and grey tones darker, not the blacks. Therefore, you don't have to be extravagant in overexposing or underexposing to get significant changes of effect.

Let's take an example. Say your light meter is telling you that ⅟₆₀ second at f/8 is the average exposure for the collected items in your composition, but you want, above all else, to capture the sunlit white wool forming a halo around a sheep. If you don't care about the other details all you have to do is close down your lens enough to render all the grey tones black. With colour film that probably will take two or three stops, so you will end up with a setting of either f/16 or f/22. The white won't be as white as it would have been if you had used f/8. But remember, since you have now eliminated all the grey tones by making them black, the rim of light on the wool has nothing to compete with for attention. In relation to the rest of the picture, the contrast has actually been increased, and the outline of the sheep will stand out dramatically. If you are using black-and-white film, choose one which produces good contrast, follow these general guidelines for colour, and make adjustments in your printing.

If you choose to reverse the procedure, the same principles apply – in reverse. Let's say that you are trying to produce an image which is delicate, airy, and light, perhaps a dewdrop sparkling on a blade of grass with the morning sun rising behind it, but the back-lighted grasses appear too dark, they conflict with your feelings about the subject. So you need to lighten the dark tones a bit. No problem. If your meter is indicating ⅟₁₀₀₀ second at f/4, you merely admit more light than the meter suggests, say ⅟₅₀₀ second at f/4. The increase in light may affect (desaturate) the colour of the sun a little, but the real effect will be on the darker tones. The sun can't get much whiter, but the grasses can certainly become less dark.

Whites, greys, blacks, light values, and exposure meters all raise again the question of tonal range. Learning to recognize differences of tone is fundamental for every photographer. Often colour photographers don't pay nearly enough attention to tone, but it's just as important as colour itself.

Indirect lighting

For me, no form of illumination is more exciting than diffused or indirect lighting. Fog, rain, clouds, and mist should not be dismissed as visual impediments, but understood as assets in the seeing and making of fine images. They don't restrict the photographer; they offer new and challenging opportunities.

Colours are richer and subtle variations of hue are more apparent on cloudy days than they are in sunshine. Best of all, there is a continuous range of tones from white to black. Gone are the searing contrasts of impenetrable blacks and scorching highlights. The blacks are still there, but reduced; the highlights are still there, but softened. If you examine a dead branch on a cloudy day, you will see that the upper side is much lighter than the underside. Light is diffused, but it still has direction, and there is plenty of contrast. The photographs on pages 13 and 95 are two of many photographs in this book that are taken with indirect lighting.

If you are photographing people in soft light, you won't have to contend with "hot spots" on their foreheads or with dark chasms where their eyes should be. You won't need fill-in flash to even up the tones. Skin colours will appear to be natural. You'll be able to photograph children playing or running and use a slow shutter speed to give a sense of motion, instead of freezing the action. You'll be able to swing or pan your camera during a horse race and capture the frenzy – not the arrested movement of a sunny day when you're forced to use either a fast shutter speed or a neutral density filter to cut down on the amount of light.

Many nature photographs are not only made more easily, but also appear more appealing and authentic when shot under diffused light. Certainly this is true with wildflowers. Colours seem to glow, hues blend gently, and glaring highlights are absent. If you see a wildflower which you want to photograph, but the sun is shining, try providing your own diffused or indirect light by shading the plant with your body.

I am not suggesting that all wildflowers must be photographed in soft light, because every photographic situation should be assessed on its own merits, but I strongly recommend this light for them. Direct lighting is far more likely to impose a dramatic pictorial effect, which may have little or nothing to do with the blossom itself. Also, the colour range is reduced in sunlight, or when you use direct flash without any reflectors to bounce light around and diffuse it. What is sensible practice when choosing light for wildflowers is even more sensible for mushrooms, a favourite subject of many nature photographers. Because many fungi prefer dark or shady places, the use of flash or strong sunlight immediately suggests a lack of authenticity.

Not all pictures of nature subjects are meant to be authentic nature photographs. Indeed, many are not. Objects in nature have always had strong symbolic values for people, and photographers may choose whatever lighting situations or other controls they want in order to strengthen the subjective statement they wish to make. Yet, even here, diffused lighting is a useful tool. No matter how selective or austere you may be in your composition, complex subtleties of tone and colour can be caught only in diffused light, and these are often powerful symbols in their own right.

White and black and intermediate shades of grey are just as important to colour photography as they are to black-and-white. A good exercise for colour photographers is to make pictures of essentially one hue, but with a wide range of tones. The placement of the bright sun and the black log protruding from the water are critical to this composition. Because the sun and the log are the same size and because both tones stand out so clearly, they function as two centres of interest. Our eyes move back and forth between them. The grey line of trees in the background interrupts this visual ping-pong game and leads us gently into other parts of the picture space.

Overexposure lightens tones and makes hues less rich. In this image I deliberately gave more exposure than the meter indicated (about ½ to ¾ an f/stop) to produce a sense of delicacy. The composition is rather complex, but the overexposure establishes a gentle mood. Most people regard flowers and dewdrops with delight; it's possible to strengthen this reaction by using the camera's controls. A morning mist also helped in this case, diffusing the sunlight and softening shadows.

Lighting conditions were virtually the same in this picture as in the one opposite, and since I wanted to convey the same sense of delicacy, I followed the same exposure plan. However, because the content of the two pictures is so different, my reasons for wanting a delicate image were not the same. The lines of the grasses that form this composition are light in tone, thin, and simple. The configuration of lines moving to a single point makes an attractive design. It was the design rather than the mood that I tried to capture.

Front lighting often produces dramatic effects when combined with underexposure, especially when the main subject reflects light while surrounding areas absorb it. Even though I made this picture shortly after sunrise, I underexposed the equivalent of three f/stops from a normal, sunny-day exposure for front-lighted subjects, shooting at $\frac{1}{125}$ second between f/16 and f/22 instead of at $\frac{1}{60}$ second between f/8 and f/11, on ISO 25 film. Actually this is probably the exposure my meter would have indicated had I metered only off the grain elevators by walking close to them and keeping the same angle of view.

The sun was high in the sky as this leaf floated by, yet my meter indicated an exposure suitable for deep shade. The reason is easy to see – much of the picture is black. The meter was accurate, but if I had followed its reading the leaf would have been washed out. I would have been fooled had I not remembered that you must take light away from a dark subject to avoid getting middle grey. The solution was to ignore the meter and simply use the film's recommended exposure for front-lighted subjects in bright sunlight.

Side lighting creates shadows which can be extremely useful in compositions. Shadows give direction, add movement, break up empty areas, and add tonal variety, so they must be placed carefully in the picture space. In this photograph they also function as secondary motifs, repeating in their long, slim shapes the basic shape of the tree. In addition, both the colour and the intensity of the light are important psychological factors. The warmth of the morning light and the softness of the shadows counteract the starkness of the basic design. Despite the fact that it's midwinter, there is no sense of the cold.

Side lighting can be used to establish accent points – centres of interest – in a composition. I looked at this chair from several angles, trying to find a point of view that would make its lines and shape stand out clearly; viewed from most positions, it seemed to fade into the surrounding architecture, which I wanted to retain in order to give scale to the chair. But from the viewpoint you see here the side lighting bounces off the shiny surface, introducing light tones and clearly delineating the structure of the chair.

Back lighting frequently creates contrast in a picture, establishing strong highlights and black areas. In this picture, our eyes move from the bright area in the foreground to the middle ground, and finally to the background. This stepladder effect establishes a tremendous sense of perspective. If your camera meter does not operate properly when you point it at the sun or at brilliantly-lighted water, try three stops of underexposure from the normal daylight setting for front-lighted subjects – as a starting point.

The lines in this photograph are similar to those in the one opposite, but here the light is diffused. The range of tones is reduced, and transitions between tones are less abrupt. The result is a more gentle impression. Few exercises can be more useful in developing one's visual perception than studying the ever-changing surface of water, looking for movement of shapes, lines, tones, and hues. Good seeing often takes time, and this exercise demands concentration before you can become fully aware of the kaleidoscope of moving forms.

Back lighting is exciting, often producing strong shadows. In this image, the grasses and, more important, their long shadows exert a strong counterforce to the horizontal movement of the straight line of sand at the bottom and the curved line at the top. As a result, our eyes have little tendency to glide out of the picture space on either the left or the right. The back lighting also introduces tonal variety to this one-colour picture, and gives a sculptured effect. It reveals the shape of the dune in a way that front lighting, and even side lighting, could not.

I was making pictures in the shade of a cliff near the ocean. It took me a long while to see the unusual purple cast produced by the reflected blue light of the water combined with the basic reddishness of the rocks. My preconceptions about how colours *should* look prevented my seeing how they *actually* looked. I immediately loaded my camera with a film that was especially sensitive to reddish-purple and reproduced it accurately. The greens in the picture were also affected by the light, but still functioned as points of colour contrast.

In this picture my preconceptions about light and colour again delayed my realizing what was in front of my eyes. Water is supposed to be blue, or grey, or black, or green, or brown – but never yellow. I actually photographed here for half an hour without seeing the colour; but when I sat down on a rock to rest, and let my eyes wander out of focus, I suddenly became aware of the swirling yellow. Immediately, I refocused my eyes – and the camera lens. The colour came from a golden maple. The photograph shows a way of seeing autumn that is all too easy to miss.

Exposure

Exposing a picture correctly is nothing more than controlling accurately the amount of light which reaches the film during a given period of time. The only correct exposure for any subject is the exposure you want. Your light meter will be an invaluable guide in measuring the intensity of light and indicating basic exposure, but it can't measure your wishes. It can't tell how bright or how dark you want the final picture to appear, so once it has told you what it can, thank it kindly for the information and then make some common sense decisions.

What can a light meter tell you?
Basically, only one thing. If it's a reflected-light meter (all meters built into cameras are of this type), you must point it at your subject; it measures the intensity of light reflected from the subject, and tells you what combinations of shutter speeds and lens openings will give you middle grey – halfway between pure white and pure black. That's what it's built for. Nothing more.

If your light meter is of the incident-light variety, you must aim it at the light source. It measures the light reaching the subject from the light source, and will tell you what combinations of lens openings and shutter speeds will produce on film the grey tones you already see in your subject.

Let's be even more specific about the difference between the two types of meters. Take two pieces of paper of identical stock, one white and one black, and place them side by side in identical light. Then, with a reflected-light meter, read the light reflected from each piece of paper, follow the meter reading indicated in each case, and you will end up with two identical photographs showing middle grey paper. Why? Because with the dark paper the reflected-light meter will tell you to admit more light for a correct exposure, and with the white paper, to reduce the light. A reflected-light meter is built to read middle grey as the correct exposure.

If you repeat the exercise with an incident-light meter, you will get one photograph which shows the black paper as black and one which shows the white paper as white. This is because the incident-light meter doesn't measure the light reflected from the two pieces of paper, but the light coming from the sun or lamp which illuminates them both.

So, doesn't the incident meter win the comparison test hands down? Not at all. It no more relieves you of final decision-making than the reflected meter, and here's why. The intensity of light a photographer sees is seldom exactly what he wants in his photograph. A photographer manipulates the brightness of light. All both meters do is provide a starting point. Then you're on your own.

Let's be specific again. It's winter and you want to photograph a field of snow. If you measure the intensity of light reflected from the snow with your reflected-light meter, and follow that measurement, you will get middle grey snow. Not very attractive. So, to put the white back into the snow, you'll have to "open up" or give more light than the meter indicates. How much extra light you give will depend on your judgement, experience, and taste. If you have an incident-light meter, you will merely follow the meter's instructions to obtain white snow.

But, let's say you want to photograph a silver-grey log which is lying in brilliant sun and which appears much brighter than you like. If you aim a reflected-light meter at the log, you will find out which camera settings will render the log middle grey. Then you simply follow what the meter says. If you point an incident-light meter at the sun, you will discover the intensity of the light falling on the log, which makes the log appear so harsh and glaring. Once you have this information, you'll have to use your own experience, judgement, and taste to determine the amount of light you want to eliminate in order to tone down the log. The incident-light meter cannot tell you how much to underexpose the log. That decision is up to you. So, in this situation, the reflected-light meter is mechanically the easier one to use.

An incident-light meter tends to be more useful than a reflected-light meter for subjects which have a preponderance of either light or dark tones, because it doesn't average the light reflected from different parts of the picture space. It isn't even aimed at them, but at the light source. A reflected-light meter tends to be more accurate in situations which have a relatively even balance of tones. However, the type of meter you have is less important than learning how to use it well.

Since most photographers use a reflected-light meter (the only type built into single-lens reflex cameras), from now on it's this type I'll be talking about. But there is no reason to be rigid about the kind of meter you use. One is not better than the other. They merely provide a photographer with different starting points.

Determining exposure

Be careful about how you hold your meter when you are measuring light. This can make the difference between a good or a poor exposure. If the main subject of your photograph is a river, point your meter at the river at precisely the same angle as your lens. Don't meter off the trees and clouds as well. If your subject is a subdued landscape, but a house stands out brightly and you don't want to overexpose it, do one or both of two things – carefully. Either meter the entire landscape to determine the average exposure for middle grey, and then "close down" to reduce exposure and take brightness out of the scene; or, meter off the house to determine exposure for middle grey, and then "open up" to put some brightness back into the house. If you try both methods, you'll find that the final exposures are very similar, if not identical.

With a reflected-light meter, once you have determined the exposure which will give you middle grey, you must "open up" or *put light back into light subjects*. You must "close down" or *take light away from dark subjects*. Read this paragraph over again. Make sure you understand it.

The really critical part of determining exposure comes after the meter has done its work. Then you're on your own, and the exciting challenges begin. Remember, the only "correct" exposure for any subject is the one you want. So you have to decide what you want and how to achieve it.

Nothing beats a little trial and error in learning what to do. You may want to bracket your exposures. Take one picture at the setting which you think is most accurate, then another which gives a little more brightness, and another which gives a little less. This is fine – for a while. But don't let it become a habit, because it can be a terrible waste of film, and it may become a crutch, an excuse which forever prevents you from achieving precise exposure control. However, if you feel that you must bracket an exposure, try doing it in one direction only. Decide if it's a little more exposure or a little less which you may require.

If you want to learn to get exact exposures, give up bracketing altogether. For two months of continuous shooting or for twenty rolls of film, permit yourself only one exposure of every picture you make. Knowing that you have to succeed with that single exposure, you will exercise a great deal of care and common sense which you may have allowed to lie dormant. The results should be dramatic. The experience, invaluable. Discipline is a great teacher.

If you want to make a note of exposures because you feel the situation is a unique learning experience, try keeping notes like these. *Photo #1* – red leaves backlighted in hazy sun, but rather dark in tone on side next to camera, gave one f/stop more light than meter indicated to brighten reds. *Photo #2* – old barn on cloudy day, light very diffused, gave one-half f/stop less exposure than indicated to darken the grey shingles slightly.

This kind of information can be used again in similar situations. Keep a record of your lens openings only when depth of field is important, and of your shutter speeds only when recording motion is important. Otherwise don't record lens openings and shutter speeds, because the information will not be relevant in another situation, where the light intensity is likely to be different.

Some photographers carry a (middle) grey card with them and take a meter reading off the card instead of off the subject. But the card is one more thing to carry, and you should learn to operate without it. If you're photographing a tiny flower against a background of dark evergreens, you'll have difficulty obtaining a meter reading from the flower. Be careful. Don't include the dark background in the area you meter. Meter the area of tone you want most, and let the dark background take care of itself, which it will. A grey card would be very handy in this situation, but you can usually find something nearby which is approximately the same tone as the flower, and you can meter off that instead of a grey card or the flower itself. Try to keep your exposure methods simple. Don't start worrying when a very simple solution is almost invariably close at hand.

Don't forget that determining exposure is a subjective matter. If, for example, you are photographing in the forest, and the trees seem almost ominous in their size and darkness, you may have to ignore what your exposure meter tells you in order to record the impact which the subject matter is making on you. Remember, you are photographing the *effect* the trees have on you just as much as the trees themselves. So, you may choose to underexpose in order to darken tones overall or to reduce some of the murkier areas to pure black. In other words, you deliberately control exposure in order to record the ominous quality.

The same procedure is often useful when photographing storms. The clouds are black and foreboding. If your meter reads (off the storm clouds) $\frac{1}{60}$ second at f/5.6, which is middle grey for that situation, and you use that exposure, you will lose all sense of the storm. Your subject will be too bright. Storm clouds are darker than middle grey. That's what gives them their impact. So, in order to get what you see and feel, reduce the amount of light reaching the film. Try $\frac{1}{125}$ second at f/5.6, or $\frac{1}{60}$ second at f/8; and if you really feel the sense of foreboding, go as far as $\frac{1}{60}$ second at f/11. What you feel about the storm should determine the correct exposure, not what you read on the light meter. The photograph on page 87 illustrates this point.

Overexposure is equally effective when your response to a subject demands desaturating colours or lightening tones throughout the picture. (See the photograph on page 62.) With snow pictures the temptation is to overreact to the brilliant light, to use too small an aperture or too fast a shutter speed, which will render snow a muddy grey colour. You must open up 1 to 1½ f/stops to put whiteness back into the snow, as I did in the photograph on page 152.

It may be useful to know that when you move from one f/stop to the next higher one (from f/8 to f/11, for example), you are cutting in half the amount of light that reaches the film. If you go the other way (from f/11 to f/8), you are doubling the light. You can also cut light in half by shooting at one shutter speed faster ($\frac{1}{125}$ second instead of $\frac{1}{60}$ second), or double the light by moving one speed in the opposite direction, that is by shooting more slowly ($\frac{1}{30}$ second instead of $\frac{1}{60}$ second, for example).

If you want an underlying guide to exposure, then keep this one in mind. When using colour films, more often than not you should choose an exposure which will render highlights accurately. When using black-and-white film, more often than not you should choose an exposure which will produce good detail in the shadow areas. Overexposure of the highlights can be corrected in the darkroom when you are making black-and-white prints, if the overexposure is not too severe. However, there is nothing you can do to add detail to shadow areas, if the negative had none in the first place.

This is the place to repeat some basic facts about exposing black-and-white films. By altering the exposure of a negative and the time it is developed, you can produce marked changes in contrast and graininess. Negatives which are underexposed and overdeveloped will show more contrast than normal. Negatives which are overexposed and underdeveloped will show less. Negatives which are both overexposed and overdeveloped will show more graininess.

Many other factors can also be brought to bear on the control of contrast in black-and-white prints, such as the kind of developer you use, the kind of paper you choose, and techniques such as dodging or burning in. These darkroom controls, along with your initial choice of film, illumination, filters, and exposure make it possible for the black-and-white photographer to have virtually complete control over contrast.

Don't throw away your exposure failures without examining them carefully. Mistakes are inevitable. But they will be useful if you take time to study what went wrong. Sometimes mistakes suggest new avenues of exploration.

Symbols and design

Symbols. The major challenge of photography is how best to describe the meeting between your subject and yourself – in other words, how to make good pictures. Nothing will be more valuable to you in meeting this challenge than an awareness of the symbolic content of your subject matter. What does it suggest to you? What does it evoke? What is it likely to suggest to others?

"To symbolize" comes from the Greek word "symballo" which, in its original sense, means "to bring together." This elementary definition is helpful for photographers, because it suggests three important ways in which a symbol "brings together."

1 / A symbol is the means by which something is made intelligible or accessible to us. It brings events or truths together in a coherent pattern. It establishes unity where otherwise there would be only a chaos of forms. A symbol does for visual composition just what it does for language, social customs, and religious ceremonies.

2 / A symbol is a meaningful centre which gives shape and pattern to the response of a person viewing a photograph, or to the beliefs and conduct of society.

3 / The most marked characteristic of a symbol is its capacity to encompass an almost limitless variety of meanings and relationships.

One might say, then, that a symbol brings unity to something not previously unified, and in doing so opens up a level of reality which would otherwise remain hidden. This has important implications for visual design, as we shall see later.

Everybody uses symbols constantly. Real communication is impossible without them. And any language, oral or visual, is only as rich as its symbolic content.

In an age where shaping and reshaping a person's image is not just a personal activity, but also big business, we regularly and deliberately try to influence others to see what we want them to see. We use symbols to do this. A symbol in itself is neither true nor false; it is a cohesive element which gives shape and pattern, enhances, and brings order to a particular reality. It makes recognition and understanding possible. Nevertheless, many symbols fail to communicate what is intended, and therefore cease to be symbols. The failure may be either with the person who sends or who receives the symbol, or with the symbol itself. Let me explain.

Blue denim jackets and jeans are rugged clothes for work and play, easy to launder, comfortable to wear, and inexpensive when compared with most other jackets and trousers. They are useful and practical clothes, but they have also become common and powerful symbols. Does a person pull on a pair of faded jeans because 1/they are the most useful and most comfortable trousers to wear under the circumstances, or 2/he believes that they connect him with a particular group of people or state of being, or 3/a person wants others to *think* that he belongs to a particular group or has a certain kind of personality, whether he actually does or not? It's sometimes very difficult to decide whether the clothes are a symbol or not, and if they are, what they symbolize or are intended to symbolize.

Pictorial composition raises many of the same problems. Many photographers use basic formulas of design which 1/may be the most appropriate to given subject matter, or 2/may be what the photographer believes to be the most appropriate, or 3/may be what the photographer wants others to think are the most appropriate because any other pictorial approach will isolate him from his photographic peers. Acceptance, with blue jeans and with pictorial composition, is often the name of the game. Wear blue jeans and be accepted in the group. Use approved formulas of composition and have your photographs accepted at the camera club. There really isn't any difference.

There are, basically, two kinds of symbols – symbols of style and symbols of content. Let me give you some examples. Why do some people commonly use vulgarities in normal conversation? In their minds, these words (symbols of content) may convey an impression of the kind of person they are. The listener may or may not understand the use of these words in the same way. If he does, the speaker is doubly successful, convincing both himself and the other person that he is, in fact, the personality he is projecting. The image and the reality are identical. If, however, the listener is offended by the language, or regards the use of these words as a "mask" or a "front," the symbols fail and so does the character projection.

Symbols of style are no less important and no less common. How a person says something is just as important as what he says. It provides just as much information. A word or phrase can be spoken in different ways and communicate very different meanings.

The serious photographer must consider the potential meanings of his symbols. First, he must ask what his subject matter (content) is likely to suggest to others. Second, he must ask what his treatment of that subject matter (style) is likely to convey. Third, he must ask if his content and style are harmonious. Is there a unity of impression? A person who proposes marriage in an angry tone of voice is using disharmonious symbols. The words (content) and the tone of voice (style) just don't go together.

A photographer's subject matter must harmonize with his style in order for the photograph to convey meaning. This fact is of paramount importance to photographers and indeed to anyone working in a visual medium. Nevertheless, it is a fact which some photographers never consider, and as a result they end up employing gimmicks and producing confusion, rather than effective visual images. Any photographic technique, such as dramatic lighting, solarization, or underexposure may help the creative photographer, but only if he carefully analyses the symbolic content of his subject and uses techniques which strengthen the content.

Symbols and design. Healthy concern for analysis does not take the joy out of photography. Quite the contrary. It helps make photography a deeply satisfying, creative adventure. It adds infinitely to one's satisfaction to deal in depth with the medium, not just to skim the surface.

A photographer should always be conscious of what the subject matter and his treatment of it suggests, both to himself and to viewers. This is one of the most important factors in picture control, and has a bearing on all other factors – choice of film, lighting, exposure, depth of field, and so on – but it has fundamental importance for pictorial composition and graphic design.

All design has the potential for symbolic effect. Photographers who intend to explore the medium in a creative way must be aware of this. They must realize that tones, hues, shapes, and lines create both physical and psychological impressions. A line which moves in a strong oblique direction across the picture space physically leads the eye. But, it also moves the mind. The viewer asks, however subconsciously, why he has been led across the space, and he must be given an answer. If the line is intended to be beautiful in its own right, the viewer should be able to perceive that. If the line points to, and thus emphasizes, another element of composition, the viewer should be able to recognize that. Obscurity in art is not a virtue.

Failure by the viewer to see what is intended is not always the photographer's fault. The viewer may not have the experience necessary to recognize the photographer's intention, which is why many artistic creations appear obscure to many people. But every artist must grapple with the problem of how his personal understanding *potentially* will be recognized.

While every serious photographer makes images to please himself, he does not make every image for this reason alone. Nobody is a complete emotional hermit. One reaches into oneself in the act of making photographs, but one also reaches out. Photography, like every other creative endeavour, exists in the tension between total self-indulgence and the need for understanding.

Design, or composition. When we talk about design or composition we are speaking, to a very large degree, about the "reaching out" of an artist toward others. This is not to say than an artist in any medium may not employ purely personal, self-directed composition, which only he understands. It's just that it's impossible to talk about this sort of composition, because it's totally personal. So, when we talk about design, we are talking about communicating.

More often than not, design is the vehicle which carries the content of an image. Less often, design is the content. When design is not the main subject of a picture, it should not be treated as if it were. It should be in keeping with the subject, but remain secondary to it.

This means, for example, that if you are photographing a scene of magnificent autumn colour, you will be sure that the person walking down the road is *not* wearing a scarlet coat. The figure, which is present merely to provide scale, should not compete for visual attention with the colour of the leaves. Similarly, the use of a stark black background and strongly dramatic side lighting in the photograph of a delicate wildflower draws attention to the strong contrasts in the image, and takes attention away from the intended centre of interest. When technique overwhelms content, the message is destroyed.

"Good design lies down quietly and behaves itself" is a useful principle and a piece of plain good sense. It is more valuable to a photographer than a good deal of specific advice about composition, such as "the ideal place for a centre of interest is ⅓ of the way from the top or bottom of the picture space, and ⅓ of the way in from either side." The first advice is a principle; the second is a formula. In artistic matters you should consider principles thoughtfully, but you should regard formulas with a healthy amount of distrust. A principle can guide you. A formula may enslave you.

The most important elements of two-dimensional visual design are: *shapes* (their size and placement); *lines* (their direction, length, and thickness); *textures* (the illusion of surface roughness and/or the weave or fabric-like structure of surface materials); *perspective* (the illusion of depth). These elements of composition are made visible by contrasts of tone and hue, which can be slightly or radically altered by changing light.

Composing a photograph is the act of organizing these elements in ways which will show your subject matter, or your feelings about it, most authentically. Good design brings order and meaning to a visual construction. It conditions the viewer to recognize that order, which means to receive your message. If your composition does not bring clarity, order, and meaning to your subject matter, it is a poor composition.

Every photographer should remember that a viewer will interpret the elements in a picture in the simplest possible way. This is Gestalt psychology's basic law of visual perception.

No matter how intricate or complex a photographic composition may be, the maker has the responsibility of organizing the details so the function of each one is integrated into the whole. The form of a photograph is its wholeness – the totality of its elements, tangible and intangible. Any discrepancy between the form and the meaning of a picture interferes with its simplicity. This is why you are more likely to make good compositions when you carefully think through the reasons for making pictures.

It's also important to remember that vision responds according to the basic laws of nature. The eye will perceive natural order, and will tend to reject unnatural arrangement or correct it automatically.

While this is a basic condition of human visual response, it doesn't mean that everybody sees things the same way. Objective and subjective order are not always identical. If they were, artistic style would be perfectly static and perfectly uniform. If you choose to stand on a rock and your friend chooses to stand in a grassy meadow in order to photograph the same landscape, each of you will see it differently and produce different perspectives of the scene, but both of you must still organize the visual elements in ways that are intelligible. Both of you must seek a basic pattern that will bring order to the complexity of shapes, lines, colours, and tones.

However, the organization of visual images requires more than attention to simplicity and basic order, because the search for simplicity leads to perfect harmony, to an absence of change, to immobility. In pictures as in life, we need tension. People crave challenge, adventure, and movement.

Life itself is an interplay of tension-heightening and tension-reducing forces. The dynamic and the static, pulling against each other, work together. Since photography has to do with life, could we possibly expect that the forces which are so basic to life would be unimportant to visual perception and to composition?

How do you put dynamics into a picture? Much of it will already be there in the form of lines and shapes which are not symmetrical and which create a sense of imbalance, force, or tension. The real question is how to make this tension work – how to organize and direct it.

The theory is fairly simple, and Rudolf Arnheim expressed it well: "The dynamics of a composition will be successful only when the 'movement' of each detail fits logically in the movement of the whole. The work of art is organized around a dominant dynamic theme, from which movement radiates throughout the entire area. From the main arteries the movement flows into the capillaries of the smallest detail. The theme struck up at the higher level must be carried through at the lower level, and elements at the same level must go together."

In practical terms, if you have an empty, static area in your picture, you may be able to alter lighting to cast oblique shadows across it. These lines will be especially useful if they lead to an important shape. Or, you may add a small dark figure to a very light, misty scene. The differences in tone and size between the figure and the rest of the picture break up the static quality; they add contrast. Contrast of any sort produces tension and makes a composition dynamic. You must be careful, however, not to add so much contrast that the mood of the picture is destroyed. In making pictorial compositions, try to assess every situation individually. Sometimes the use of different colours and the amount and placement of them will produce the tension you need. At other times you will depend on lines, shapes, or tones. Do your best to avoid repeating the same solution time after time.

Only a small amount of good sense about design can be taught. The rest grows in a person. However, here are some basic problems and solutions to consider. To strengthen a shape you may 1/increase its size by moving closer to it; 2/make it lighter or darker in tone than surrounding shapes; or 3/place it at the end of a leading line or convergence of lines.

To gain a greater sense of space in a composition, you may 1/increase the size of empty areas such as sky; 2/reduce the size of your main subject; or 3/introduce lines which appear to lead away from the foreground into the background.

To avoid confusion in a visual image, you may 1/reduce the number of elements in the picture space, especially the number of different elements; 2/emphasize a single object while de-emphasizing other objects, so the viewer's eye no longer moves rapidly from one visual element to another; or 3/deliberately include lines or forms which repeat the direction, shape, hue, or tone of the main subject, but which in themselves are less noticeable.

However, it is not sufficient merely to know how to strengthen shape, gain a greater sense of space, or avoid confusion; you must determine why you want to do these things. You should have reasons for each decision you make about composition, if you want the design of your image to convey your intended message. In the captions for the photographs on pages 85 to 96, I share with you my thoughts and decisions about symbolism and design that influenced the making of each image.

You will gain experience in design, not only by making and viewing pictures, but also by studying all the visual media. When you're at the theatre, notice the arrangement of the set and the way the director has blocked the action. If you're a fan of modern dance or ballet, watch the movement and flow of the dance, and note its relevance to photographic composition. As you amble through a gallery, study not only the paintings and sculpture on display, but also how the director has arranged them in the available space and in relation to one another. In short, use your eyes all the time. Photography does not begin when you pick up your camera, and learning about design should not end when you put it down. The challenges and the opportunities to learn are endless. Take advantage of them as often as you can.

This jacket confronts most of us with indisputable impact. I think it represents a symbol to many people, which is why I chose a point of view that is direct and uncluttered by any other visual details. It's the simplest possible composition. The jacket is strong enough to stand by itself visually, and for some people, emotionally. Are you repelled by thoughts of motorcycle gangs? Or are you attracted, either by a sense of force and strength, or by the vitality of bold shape and colour? Simplicity in composition can lead to simplicity, clarity, and impact in communication.

Although I spent a day with this man, I didn't get to know him well. He was uncommunicative, brooding, hidden from me. Late in the afternoon when we sat down for tea, I had a camera with me. As he leaned forward into a shaft of light I reacted instantly, and this photograph is the result. I'm pleased with the picture because it shows the man as I experienced him – mostly hidden, unwilling to reveal much about himself. The large areas of black in the photograph and the shadow falling across his eyes reinforce the unknown, visually and symbolically.

The lines of light on the ocean seem about to vanish. Is a dark and raging storm moving across the water, or is the curtain of night about to fall? There is a sense of impending doom. Because the darkness conveyed so much, I made two critical decisions: to underexpose drastically in order to preserve the black, and to keep the lines of light near the bottom of the picture so the sky area would seem overwhelming. Composition should be determined by picture content, rather than be imposed upon it. It's far better to have reasons for each composition you make, than to have rules which you try to force upon the subject.

Photographers sometimes have a tendency to move too close to a centre of interest. While this may reveal physical details of the main subject more clearly, it reduces the environmental space, which is often a great loss. The relatively small area occupied by the sheep and the large area given over to converging lines create a strong sense of perspective and scale in this picture. The placement of the sheep is most important. They form a visual anchor or balance to the strong pull of lines leading our eyes out of the picture at the upper right.

Careful examination of tones, especially highlights and dark areas, is essential
for good design. Except for the line of green grass, this image is composed
mostly of shades of grey. However, there are solid blacks in the hubs of the
wheels, and highlights in the wagon, particularly on the upper rims of the front
wheels. Nothing in the composition is more important than the highlights on the
front wheels. At first I stood more to the left, but that put the lightest tones on the
rear wheels, making the wagon appear to be sliding backwards. So I inched to
the right until the highlights shifted to the front wheels.

As I drove along an isolated country road in southern Africa, these people got off a bus in front of me and set off over the hills toward their village, singing in four-part harmony. The joy of their music and the colour of their clothes gave me a tremendous exuberance, and I thought I could show this in the picture by giving the sky prominence, perhaps because happiness implies "looking up." My decision to emphasize the sky was instinctive, and I still feel it was the right approach.

The design is the content in this photograph. Repeated colours, shapes, and lines had to be organized in a pleasing way within the picture space, and in a very short time, because I was flying over the slag heaps quite quickly. Most important was the placement of the three red buildings. When I pressed the shutter release, they moved my eye across the picture from lower right to upper left. This invisible line which they suggest crosses the visible lines in the picture and ties them together, bringing unity to the composition.

This stairway is in the East Block of the Parliament Buildings in Ottawa, and is illuminated by both daylight and tungsten lights. I felt it was important to have all the picture elements as sharply in focus as possible, so I focused along the top railing and used maximum depth of field. The 35mm lens allowed me to show the entire staircase. It's a purely documentary image. What pleases me is the way the railings and the cool lights surround and enclose the warm colours.

The two most important aspects of design in this photograph are the highlights on the curving backs and seats of the church pews, and the colours reflected in the seats. The curving lines give the picture basic order and pattern. The colours lift the picture out of the documentary class – aesthetically and symbolically. It's very easy to miss pictures like this one, because it's difficult to be constantly aware of details. Learning to see what is in front of our eyes demands concentration and constant practice.

Some images do not require a centre of interest and would be spoiled if they had one. The autumn leaves floating on a small pond create a tapestry, weaving together the colours of the season. Full depth of field is essential here, because if any of the leaves are out of focus they will be distracting. Also it is important to note how much black is in the picture – perhaps twenty-five percent of the total area. The black affects the meter reading, indicating less light than is actually available, so underexposure (about ½ an f/stop, or a little more) is necessary to retain the richness of the colours.

This composition forced me to impose order. The yellow ferns were attractive, but pointed in so many directions that no coherent pattern emerged. By carefully searching for a point of contrast, I discovered the purple and green blackberry leaves. The ferns occupy most of the picture space, but their function here is to provide a context for the brightly-coloured leaves. Order is achieved both visually and mentally. The diffused lighting brings out the subtle hues. Strong shadows and bright highlights of direct sunlight would have competed for attention.

Few subjects have as much symbolic content for so many people as the rising sun, especially when its rays stream through an early mist. Successful composition here depended on accurate exposure, because if the tones had been too dark or too light the rays' effect could have been destroyed. My meter was only a rough guide, and I chose my exposure by a process of elimination and common sense. The back lighting was much brighter than normal front lighting on sunny days but, because of the mist, not as bright as direct light from an unclouded sun. An exposure midway between these reference points yielded acceptable results.

Point of focus and depth of field

Still photography is a two-dimensional medium, but focus and depth of field have to do almost exclusively with the apparent third dimension – depth. A sense of depth is critical in the design of most photographs. Therefore choosing a point of focus and deciding upon the depth of field you want are among the most fundamental aspects of composing a photograph. However, they deserve consideration apart from other elements of composition, because depth of field is related to exposure and is not purely a matter of design.

To put it simply, the point of focus is that subject in your picture on which you focus your lens. The depth of field is the span of distance in front of and behind the point of focus which appears fully sharp. Regardless of the lens you are using and no matter what you are focused on, depth of field is greatest at minimum apertures (f/22, f/16) and shallowest at maximum apertures (f/1.4, f/2.8).

With every lens and every lens opening you select, the depth of field (except for extreme close-ups) extends forward ⅓ of its distance from the point of focus, and backward ⅔ of its distance. To put it another way, there's always twice as much depth of field behind the point of focus as in front of it.

Choosing depth of field

If you are using a 50mm lens, and not making any close-ups, you could simply set the point of focus at about 4½ metres and not bother to change it much. If you use a reasonably small aperture (f/22, f/16, or f/11), you can be certain that everything behind the focal point will appear sharp, and that the apparent sharpness will extend forward from the point of focus to about 2, 2½, or 3 metres from the lens. This should cover everything you want in focus. Maximum depth of field was used in the photograph on page 92.

If you always wanted as much depth of field as you could get, there would be no large lens openings, no problems, and no chapter on the subject in this book. But, that's not the case. Sometimes the subject matter virtually dictates that you reduce or limit depth of field; and at other times you will decide on restricted depth of field for purely personal reasons.

The need for maximum depth of field is usually self-evident. You view the total picture area, and feel that having any part of it out of focus will be distracting. On other occasions you will view the picture area and decide that having anything besides the main subject in sharp focus will be distracting, so you will choose minimum depth of field, as I did in the photograph on page 19.

Because these decisions are often easy ones to make does not mean that they are unimportant. Photographs, like medicines, do not necessarily have to be difficult to take in order to be effective. If you decide quickly on the depth of field you want, don't automatically assume that you're visually naive or that you should fuss about awhile longer. It may, instead, be an indication of your growing expertise in assessing visual impact and pictorial effect.

Nevertheless, the real test comes with the intermediate f/stops, that is, with partially restricted depth of field. Deciding between f/11 and f/8 is rather like deciding between one bay leaf or two for the pot of soup you're making. The finest flavours result from the most subtle adjustments to the recipe. Well, how do you decide?

The matter should be considered both negatively and positively. Let's examine the negative approach first. Certain compositions fail because some elements in the picture are visually bothersome. Perhaps showing through the trees is a spot of light sky which pulls your eye away from the clump of ferns you're photographing, simply because it's so much lighter in tone than the ferns. You cannot alter the position of your camera to eliminate the bright spot without ruining the rest of your composition, so you reduce the impact of that bright spot by pressing your depth-of-field preview button, and then moving to successively wider lens openings until the spot is diffused enough (out of focus) to stop being a distraction. Meanwhile, because the ferns are the objects on which you focused in the first place, they will remain sharp and clear. This is the negative approach to deciding on depth of field – a way to improve composition by eliminating distractions, or by reducing them at least. It's an important basic method and frequently must be used along with the positive approach.

The positive approach to determining depth of field can be stated simply. Assuming there are no major distractions in the picture space, you select the depth of field which produces the suitable degree of emphasis on your main subject or on the total impact of the image. Such a decision demands personal judgements. A teacher of photography can easily spot a bad decision; he should also be able to recognize the near misses and help to correct them. But, in the end, the student cannot rely on somebody else's feelings and advice. He or she must make the final choice. As you look at the image you are composing, you must remember to value your own instincts. You must be willing not only to think, but also to say, "This depth of field *feels* right to me." Then you must press the shutter release, and later examine the results.

In learning about depth of field, look for guidance from your camera club, your photographer friends, magazine articles, and from viewing pictures. But don't look for formulas. Like so much else in photography, selecting depth of field becomes part of your style, your personal statement of who you are and how you respond. Every time you choose a formula over a personal decision, you are denying a part of yourself.

The negative and positive approaches frequently coincide. Often your potential image confronts you with two problems – how to reduce the effect of distracting elements and how to select the depth of field which is most compelling. Sometimes you cannot solve both problems simultaneously, and eventually have to admit defeat and select a new image. While you may be disappointed about this, don't be downhearted.

The chances are quite good that you can find a solution in most cases, or at least achieve a compromise which you can live with. The whole business of trying is, in itself, an education in composition. Try shifting the point of focus, and viewing the composition at the various f/stops. Shift again, view again. And again. Keep at it until you've exhausted the possibilities or discovered the best combination.

Don't forget that you can pause at points between the f/stops on your lens – and you should whenever your selection of depth of field or exposure calls for minute adjustment. There will be many times when f/8 is almost right and f/11 is almost right, but halfway between the two is exactly right. Don't think of your lens as a piece of equipment with six or seven adjustable settings. Think of it as a continuum, as an infinitely variable apparatus which has only two restrictions, one at each end of the f/stop scale. And remember, all of this is much easier to think about and to do when you have your camera on a tripod.

At the beginning of this section, I said that depth of field is not just a matter of design, but is related to exposure, and that depth of field influences the sense of perspective or third dimension in an image. Let's look at these two statements in turn.

Exposure and depth of field
When you are composing most images, choosing your f/stop (that is, choosing

your depth of field) is far more important than choosing your shutter speed. Only after you have settled on the depth of field and selected an f/stop should you read your meter and select the shutter speed which will give you a satisfactory exposure at that f/stop.

There are some important exceptions to this principle. For example, you may have a strong preference for photographing flowing water at very slow shutter speeds – the longer the better. In most lighting situations this forces you to use a small aperture, usually f/22 (unless you have a neutral density filter). Therefore, you have to live with maximum depth of field, and simply make certain that having every picture element in clear focus doesn't mean including any distracting features.

Hues are not rendered the same at every shutter speed. You will not get the same yellow at ⅛ second as you will at ¹⁄₅₀₀ second. Try out your lenses with various colour films at the different shutter speeds. You'll have to discover with your own equipment what the tendencies of the colour shift are, and you'll have to decide if they are significant enough to bother you. (See also "Films," pages 45 and 46.) If they are, consider reading a manual on the use of filters in colour photography, and perhaps buy a filter or two.

The perception of depth
What is the influence of depth of field on a sense of depth in your images? What about the perspective of depth? While other factors of composition (such as lines and shapes) affect all three dimensions, the primary impact of any given depth of field is on the depth perspective only. This is why I've separated it from other elements of design.

Do not assume that the picture with the greatest depth of field will automatically convey the greatest impression of depth to the viewer. A line which begins in the foreground and leads off into the distance may appear longer to some viewers if it becomes increasingly out of focus as it moves toward the background, than if it remains sharp. This perception may be a learned one, or it may be a purely individual response. Whichever it is, the photographer should extract a principle from it – that many visual constructions say more by what they suggest than by what they show.

So, once again, choosing depth of field enters the realm of subjectivity. All human beings do not have the same perception of depth. Some of the images which I most enjoy are those which lack a precise definition of depth, and which allow me to shift my visual and mental viewpoint while looking at them. The uncertainty of visual perception will frustrate you only if you are looking for formulas or rules in order to operate. Most of the time it should excite and challenge you.

Making Pictures

The importance of using your camera

The most important thing you can do with your camera and lenses is to use them. Reading books and taking photographic courses can be very useful, but they can't begin to approach the value and pleasure of using your equipment regularly. A typist soon loses her speed if she doesn't use her typewriter frequently. A photographer loses his ability to make precise exposures if he packs his gear away once the leaves have fallen off the trees. And worse still, if you do this you stop growing as a photographer. Your knowledge of the craft suffers. Your ability to visualize keenly begins to stagnate.

A few years ago a friend and I built a house, working away through autumn into winter. Most mornings when I climbed up on the roof, the air was frigid. Frost lay on black shingles like peppermint icing on a chocolate cake. On the mornings when there wasn't any frost, there was often snow. I brushed it off the dormers and the staging so I could get to work, pausing occasionally to view the white-wreathed cedars from a favourable vantage point.

The photographer's eye was always at work, though sometimes with disastrous results. I acquired a multitude of blood blisters, every one agonizing testimony to the fact that I was looking at the scenery when I should have been watching my hammer. But, I learned! I learned that I could be a carpenter and a photographer at the same time. I discovered that there is time to make pictures every day, no matter how busy I am.

Most amateurs don't take a camera to work with them, and for the first few days of being a carpenter, neither did I. Very foolish of me, because most of those missed opportunities won't come again. I'm not sure what made me wake up, maybe a particularly lovely sunrise through the snowy spruce or the pattern of afternoon light on the rows of roof beams. But I do know that, before long, I picked up a camera every morning along with my saws, hammer, and nails.

Having a camera with me, even when the whole day was devoted to building, was a very healthy thing. It's known as being prepared. Nobody works for eight or ten hours without stopping, not even me. There was lunch at least, and usually a short break for a thermos of hot coffee. Wandering around with coffee in one hand and a camera in the other was a lot more relaxing than just sitting on my fanny. It was a total diversion, a complete change. Added to that was the fact that I did get quite a few good pictures during these short respites. I would go back to work ten or fifteen minutes later feeling that I was not a captive to my job, that it hadn't utterly consumed my day or my spirit.

What's possible for a carpenter is just as possible for the photographer who's a truck driver, a secretary, or a meteorologist. Having a job with regular hours doesn't mean that you can never make pictures during those hours. To begin with, there's lunch hour. Most people don't spend much time eating, but use the break for shopping, or reading the newspaper, or just chatting. It's a perfect time to make pictures – and the change can do wonders for your spirit. Leave your tripod behind at first; take your camera and only one lens. Pick just one subject for the half-hour you have available – reflections in windows, shadows, a school-crossing guard helping small children – but choose a subject which appeals to you. The next day try the same subject again, but with another lens. Stay with your subject until you find yourself wanting to turn to other things.

If it's raining heavily, set up your tripod in the office. Try still-life arrangements of books, pencils, and office equipment. Work on the patterns of water on the windowpanes. Shoot down at the street to catch people hurrying by in their brightly-coloured raincoats and umbrellas. If your fellow workers think you've gone slightly crazy, don't let it bother you. In a couple of days, they'll ignore you. But after a month or so, invite a few of them to your home for an evening and put on a show of the slides you've made during lunch hours. From that point on, they'll be coming to you with suggestions, and you'll also find it easy to make photographs of them.

By shooting a few minutes every day, you will develop your photographic skills, increase your ability to see good images, and soon have an extensive collection of slides or negatives. In fact, once you start photographing during lunch hours and coffee breaks, you'll probably make more pictures than you ever will if you wait until you get home, because all the good intentions you had during the day will have dissipated by the time you plop yourself down in an easy chair. If you don't carry a camera to work, you can go for months without ever making a picture. And to experience the joy of being a photographer you have to make pictures.

Experimenting with selective focus

Selective focus is an important technique directly related to depth of field. Strictly speaking, every photographer uses selective focus every time he makes a picture. He chooses a point or plane in the picture area on which to focus, and then he selects either 1/a small lens opening, such as f/16 or f/22, which will keep all other picture detail pretty well in focus, or 2/a larger lens opening, such as f/3.5 or f/8, which will throw some of the picture out of focus. However, in popular usage, selective focus has come to mean the latter – the use of a wide aperture to achieve a very shallow depth of field, a definition I shall use here. Several photographs in this book have been made with this technique, for example, on pages 16 and 127.

Some photographers use selective focus to achieve particular effects, such as softening harsh lines, blending background colours, or making the centre of interest stand out distinctly from other elements in the composition.

A few use it to create certain moods or patterns. The photographer who uses it well usually has considered its purpose carefully. No technique, in itself, has any intrinsic value. The value comes in its being applied successfully, to accomplish the photographer's aims.

But let's discuss a specific example of selective focus.

Imagine a vast field of daisies stretching away from your feet to a deep green forest. In the field, about halfway between you and the woods, a group of children is playing. Basically, you have three areas or planes in this situation. 1/a *foreground* of daisies; 2/a *middle ground* with the children and the flowers immediately around them; and 3/a *background* of trees.

You may want to use a lens opening of f/22 and put every part of the scene in sharp focus. On the other hand, you may feel like creating a dreamlike atmosphere, a special feeling of summer, or a nostalgic look at a summer of your memory. If so, selective focus may be your best answer, and here are three different ways to try it.

1 / You may wish to focus on the foreground, and use a wide lens opening, such as f/2.8. This will keep the nearest daisies sharp, but will soften the detail of the children and the daisies around them, and the background as well. The children will appear, not as recognizable images, but as figures of children. The forest beyond will become a soft, green backdrop. Such an image may have far more allure than a photograph which is in focus from front to back.

2 / You could crouch down and shoot through the daisies, but switch your focus to the middle ground, where the children are playing. With the same wide lens opening, the foreground flowers will now become blurs of white and gold dancing across the picture. Through them the children may be seen sharp and clear, but almost as if they were in a dream. Behind, the forest will still be a soft green backdrop.

3 / You might focus only on the forest background, although the effect in this case may not be very strong. However, in other cases, throwing both foreground and middle ground out of focus, while keeping the background sharp, is very effective indeed. In Dawson City, once, I wanted to photograph the outside wall of a log cabin. However, as I looked through the viewfinder, I found the lines of the old logs too strong and straight for my liking. I wanted to soften them, to induce a visual element which would make the logs seem a memory, or a symbol of memory. So, I backed away through a tiny field of fireweed. Then, taking a low camera position, I aimed through the fireweed, but focused on the logs of the cabin. The out-of-focus pink circles of fireweed in the foreground softened the overall pattern sufficiently to eliminate the harshness in my original composition, and introduced a new and suggestive element, an intangible sort of colour and shape. I was presenting a cabin somewhat dimly seen, somewhat obscured, clouded, if you like, by the passage of time.

Selective focus may be achieved with any lens, but for most photographers it comes more easily with a lens longer than 50mm, because with longer lenses the depth of field appears to be so much shallower than it does with the standard lens at the same opening. Also, close-up equipment is very useful for creating selective focus, because the closer the subject you are focused on, the less depth of field you have.

One of my favourite times for working with this technique is at sunset, especially on a night when the sun is a huge red orb descending through a misty sky. I race for my 100mm macro lens, or for some other close-up equipment, and then plop myself down in the middle of a field of long grass. Quickly I extend the lens to minimum focusing distance, about 15 centimetres, and set it at its widest aperture. This combination gives me an extremely narrow depth of field.

When I point my camera to view the setting sun, something fantastic happens! Because the sun is completely out of focus, it is tremendously enlarged and fills much of the picture space. A circle becomes a bigger circle when it's thrown out of focus, and the more it's out of focus the bigger it becomes.

But that's not all. As I crawl through the grass, individual blades of grass, flowers, and seed heads brush against the lens, passing from out of focus to in focus then out again. When a grass or combination of grasses forms a delicate composition against the backdrop of the huge red sun, I pause and carefully inch forward or backward until I'm satisfied I have the best arrangement possible. Then I press the shutter release.

To get this effect, remember that 1/you must use the widest lens opening (nothing else), because otherwise the out-of-focus sun will appear hexagonal, not round, and it will not fill as much of the picture area; 2/you must leave the lens at minimum focusing distance, because this also enlarges the sun, and move slightly forward or backward to get the point of focus precisely where you want it.

Since the lens is at maximum aperture and admitting a great deal of light, your meter will indicate a very fast shutter speed, probably starting at $\frac{1}{1000}$ second when the sun is still well above the horizon and moving down to $\frac{1}{60}$ second as the sun sets. The choice of shutter speed will depend on the intensity of the sun at any time and on the flowers or grasses in front of your lens, which are preventing some of the sunlight from entering the lens.

If you own a single-lens reflex camera, you'll find experimenting with selective focus and shallow depth of field very easy, since you'll be able to see in the viewfinder precisely what is in focus and what is not, and thus, by varying lens openings you can choose the effect of greater or lesser depth of field.

Real competence with selective focus takes practice. It's easy, but it's difficult too. You may be pleased with the results of your attempts, but the more practice you get the more likely you will be to achieve precise control in many kinds of situations. If you are keen to grasp the visual opportunities offered by this technique, stay with it. Challenge any preconceptions you have about focusing and depth of field.

Showing motion in still pictures

There are times when every photographer wishes he had a movie camera on his tripod, because he feels what's happening would be shown better in motion than in still pictures. Times like this can be frustrating, especially if you're not familiar with some of the techniques available for conveying movement and activity. Several possibilities are available, so let's explore them and try them. The more ways you can show movement, the more interesting your picture sequences will be.

Oblique lines
Oblique lines are dynamic lines. Unlike horizontal lines (which suggest rest and peacefulness) or vertical lines (which imply dignity, formality, and stiffness), oblique lines move the viewer's eye quickly across the picture space. They suggest that something is happening, as in the photograph on page 63.

When you're photographing a horse race or a child running, watch for those moments when bodies are on a tilt, leaning forward or into a curve. Capture the imbalance. This won't make the child or the horse look as if it were about to fall over, but rather will create a strong sense of activity in the viewer's mind, and he'll have no trouble understanding what's going on.

Peak action
In many sports there comes a moment when the competitor reaches the zenith of his effort and seems to hang briefly in the air – high jumping and pole vaulting are good examples. The trick is to press the shutter release a split second before the peak of action. If you wait for the pole-vaulter to reach his highest point before releasing the shutter, you'll find you've missed the critical moment. Peak action photographs are usually very successful, because viewers instinctively imagine

everything you can't show – the powerful lunge before the leap and the "thud" to the ground which follows it. The photograph on page 147 shows that shooting peak action is not limited to sports events.

Slow shutter speeds and time exposures

Slow shutter speeds cause the blurring of any objects in your picture which are travelling faster than the shutter itself, as you can see in the photograph on page 129. The slower the speed (i.e., the longer the exposure), the greater the blur, and the more pronounced the sense of movement. If two objects in the picture are moving at the same speed, the one nearer the camera will appear to be more blurred.

A slow shutter speed, let's say $\frac{1}{30}$ or $\frac{1}{15}$ second, captures a snowstorm well. It's slow enough to make every flake into a short white streak, but it's fast enough to stop the blizzard from looking like a downpour of rain. This is shown in the photograph on page 135. Another technique for a snowstorm, especially effective when combined with a slow shutter speed, is to fire a flash gun during the exposure. This illuminates flakes close to the lens brilliantly and arrests them in midair. You get a very snowy picture – a real eye-stopper! And it's easy because you don't have to bother calculating exposure for the flash. Just stick with the shutter speed and lens opening you've already chosen for the scene.

A slow shutter speed will give a sense of softness to falling or flowing water, as in the photograph on page 137. Apparently the eye sees motion at about $\frac{1}{15}$ second, so if you photograph a waterfall faster than that you'll make it appear frozen, particularly if the water is falling very gently. (The faster the rush of water, the faster the shutter speed required to freeze it.) When you use a slower shutter speed, you'll increase the blur of water and induce a misty quality.

The swirl of water and foam created by waves breaking on a beach are recorded far more accurately at a slow shutter speed, say $\frac{1}{4}$ second, than at speeds of $\frac{1}{60}$, $\frac{1}{125}$, or $\frac{1}{250}$ second. However, a long exposure, perhaps 30 seconds at twilight will transform a raging sea into a completely calm body of water. During such a long exposure many waves will traverse the picture space, but because of the low light they will not be recorded as waves at any point. This is using a time exposure (any exposure longer than one second) to stop or eliminate movement altogether, and the results can be soft and lovely.

A time exposure can create the impression of movement as well. If you are shooting during the evening and aim your lens at a street or expressway, it makes sense to try a long exposure in order to record the headlights and tail-lights of cars moving across the picture space. The speed of the vehicles is important; note how long it takes two or three of them to move through your composition, then expose the film for at least that duration. The longer you expose, the more likely you are to record more moving lights, so you may want to use a small lens opening (f/16 or f/22) to prevent overexposing the scene. If there are a few moments when no cars are passing, simply put your hand in front of the lens. If it's dark, the film won't record your hand, and you will prevent overexposure of areas in the picture which are illuminated by streetlights.

Panning

Panning is a simple technique for giving the effect of motion in still photographs. It keeps the main subject relatively sharp while blurring the background, thus giving the impression that the subject is passing rapidly through the picture area. The photograph on page 130 shows the effect you get by panning. It is so simple, and usually so successful, that photographers trying it for the first time are often amazed at the results. Here's how you do it.

First, you get ready. 1/Any camera or lens will do, but a 100mm lens or longer is best, unless you're very close to the moving object. 2/Choose a slow-speed or medium-speed film (ISO 25, 50, or 64), unless the light level is low or you have a neutral density filter, because panning is usually done at $\frac{1}{15}$ or $\frac{1}{30}$ second. If you're using ISO 200 or 400 film, you'll be overexposing at $\frac{1}{15}$ or $\frac{1}{30}$ second in bright light, since most lenses don't stop down beyond f/16 or f/22. 3/Pre-focus on the area where the subject will be when you actually make the picture; then don't worry about adjusting the focus again.

Now you are ready to make the picture. 1/Pick up the moving object in your viewfinder and follow it as it approaches. 2/As it passes through the area on which you pre-focused, press the shutter release, but don't stop following the moving object. Keep swinging, just as a baseball player follows through with his bat once he has hit the ball. If you don't follow through, you'll invariably stop swinging before you actually press the shutter release, and get no effect of motion at all. And that's all there is to it!

Zooming

If you have a zoom lens, you'll find it comes in handy for implying movement where none is taking place. In zooming, all sorts of oblique lines of colour and tone emanate from the centre of the picture and travel toward the edges (or vice versa). For example, focus on a maple tree in full autumn colour, and zoom your lens (extend or reduce the focal length) during an exposure of $\frac{1}{15}$ to 1 second. The result – an explosion of colour, as in the photograph on page 128.

Here's how you do it. 1/Set your camera and lens on a tripod, if possible, as this will make the operation easier. 2/Choose a slow-speed or medium-speed film (ISO 25, 50, or 64) unless the light level is quite low or you have a neutral density filter, because you should zoom at shutter speeds of $\frac{1}{15}$ second or longer. It's difficult manually to complete the zooming any faster than that. 3/Set your lens at the smallest aperture (f/16 or f/22) in order to reduce the light reaching the film. This will also help you to make a longer exposure. 4/Compose your picture twice – once at the maximum range of your lens and once at the minimum. If your lens is an 80 – 200mm zoom, compose your image at 80mm and again at 200mm. The composition at 80mm will cover a greater subject area, so at this lens position be certain there is nothing in the picture which is distracting or undesirable. 5/With your lens set at either 80mm or 200mm, press the shutter release. As you press the release, or a fraction of a second before, use your other hand to extend the lens very quickly from 80mm to 200mm, or to retract it from 200mm to 80mm during the exposure. This is called zooming.

You won't be able to pre-visualize the final effect, but the more zoomed pictures you make, the more accurate you will become in predicting the kind of results you'll achieve; you will learn when zooming is likely to work well.

Rotating the lens
Many long lenses come with a collar attached. The collar allows you to screw the head of your tripod into the lens, rather than into the camera. This is important, because long lenses are often heavy and will cause a tripod to upset if they are not attached to it near their centre of gravity. The collar also has a screw in it which, when loosened, allows you to rotate your lens and camera from the horizontal to the vertical position without touching anything else.

You can use the lens collar in a way for which it was not intended – and the visual effects can be very striking. You can rotate your camera and lens during an exposure – in much the same fashion as zooming. But, instead of getting oblique lines emanating from the centre of the picture, you'll have concentric circles of colour and tone revolving around it.

Here are the steps to follow. 1/Affix your camera and lens to a tripod by screwing the head of the tripod into the collar of the lens. 2/Select a low-speed or medium-speed film (ISO 25, 50, or 64) unless the light is weak, because you will need to rotate the camera and lens at a slow shutter speed in order to complete the rotation during the exposure. 3/Set your lens at the smallest aperture (f/16 or f/22) in order to reduce the amount of light reaching the film. This will also help you to make a longer exposure. 4/Compose your picture twice. First, try the camera in a vertical position (or the horizontal position, it doesn't matter). Then, release the screw in the lens collar which keeps the lens and camera from moving, and rotate the camera to the other position. Check the new composition carefully. Are there any distracting elements in either composition? If not, leave the camera in either the vertical or horizontal position. 5/Do not tighten the collar screw. Leave the camera and lens free for rotation. 6/Press the shutter release, and as you press, use your other hand to rotate the camera and lens quickly – during the exposure.

As with zooming, you won't be able to pre-visualize the final effect exactly, but practice will improve your ability to predict the result, and you will be able to achieve a good deal of control.

This technique is even more effective if you make a double exposure. Make the first shot normally, but use only half the calculated exposure. (If your meter indicates 1 second at f/22, expose at ½ second at f/22.) Make the second shot at the same exposure as the first, but this time rotate the camera and lens during the exposure. The combination of reality and unreality creates an aura of mystery. You can even try zooming and rotating at the same time, or making a double exposure – one zoomed and one rotated. It takes manual dexterity and concentration, but – wow!

Sequential shooting

Since slides are usually shown one after another, you can convey activity through sequential shooting and presentation. It won't work for waterfalls, but it will work for kids and sports of all kinds, and it will probably work best if you employ some of the techniques I've just described.

A short, snappy sequence projected quickly usually conveys action best, but the speed at which you project will depend on your subject matter. If you are showing the approach, leap, and fall of a high-jumper, you may want to cycle your slides very quickly. If you are showing a sequence of ballet steps, you will probably want to project more slowly, so viewers can appreciate the grace of the dancer's movements.

If you're thinking of a photo sequence, be fairly liberal in your shooting and very tough in your editing. A story which can be told in ten pictures will rarely be improved if it's told in twenty. Examine your photographs carefully to see which images and what order convey the action most clearly and succinctly. The beauty of a sequence is that you can build to a climax; so be sure nobody falls asleep before you reach it.

Using flash

In no other area of camera technology do improvements and variations in equipment seem to come with such rapidity as they do with flash units. The average photographer can't keep up with them, nor should he try.

The time to start thinking about what kind of flash you should buy is when you find yourself restricted because you don't have one. Before you go near a camera store, do two things. First, try to evaluate your own needs. What do you want a flash to do for you? How often are you likely to use flash? Do you ever take more than a roll of photographs which require flash – at any one time? Do you ever need to illuminate large areas at night, or will a flash that lights an object up to six or seven metres away be satisfactory? Do you want a unit which measures exposure for you, or would you prefer total personal exposure control?

Each photographer will have to answer these questions for himself, but once you've answered them, try to find the lightest, most compact, and least expensive unit which will do the job you want.

The second thing you should do before making a purchase is to examine what other photographers are using. Ask a friend to demonstrate his equipment. Remember that anybody who has already made a purchase is likely to justify the wisdom of his choice. Be appreciative, but cautious. Next, try to make comparisons with flash units other friends own. Look for the following features. 1/a variable position head; 2/a wide-angle to telephoto adjustment; 3/variable power output; 4/capacity for manual and automatic operation; 5/a sensor that can be connected to an extension cord for precise exposure reading; and 6/a built-in filter holder. Now you're in a good position to ask your dealer intelligent questions.

Once you buy a flash, use it right away. Try it out in different situations. Get used to it. Don't wait until you *need* to use it before you make pictures with it. In short, start immediately to overcome any fears you may have about using it, especially if you are naturally intimidated by new equipment. What you want is another tool for effective picture control, and control comes with practice and familiarity.

With many 35mm cameras you are instructed to use a given shutter speed, often $\frac{1}{60}$ second, when using electronic flash. While you must not use a faster shutter speed, there is nothing to prevent you from using a slower one. The flash will do its work just as effectively, and the extra exposure time will add more available light to distant areas not affected by the flash. If you do use a faster speed than what is recommended, part of your picture will be black.

Flash has application in photography both as a main light source and as a secondary one. When you use it as a main source, keep in mind what you've learned about front, side, and back lighting, all of which are forms of direct illumination. With front lighting the shadow will fall behind your subject. So, if your model is very close to a wall, the shadow may appear in the picture or it may disappear behind your subject. This can be either an asset or a liability, depending on the intended composition. If you want to eliminate a background shadow, you can move your model away from the wall or use bounce flash. With bounce flash you direct the light toward a nearby reflecting wall or object, rather than pointing it directly at your subject. The light which bounces back from the reflecting surface will be scattered or diffused, and will enable you to achieve the gentle lighting effects of a cloudy day. Read your instruction booklet to learn how to estimate exposure with your particular unit.

Flash is also important as a secondary source of illumination. You can use it to light up dark corners or objects if you want detail in these areas. The most common example is using flash to light up the face of a back-lighted person whose face is darker than surrounding objects. (This is known as fill-in flash.) But, it's just as valuable when you're photographing people who are standing in bright sunlight, because their eyes are likely to be in deep shadow.

If the main source of illumination is strong, you will probably want to calculate your exposure for the entire scene, and place your flash at a distance from the object to be filled in, which will bring out its detail without making it brighter than surrounding material.

Very often you can use flash as both a primary and secondary source of illumination. One flash unit is used as the main source of light and the second is used to fill in areas not illuminated by the first. Many portrait photographers regularly use two or more flash units, and so do photographers of botanical subjects who don't want to rely on available light. Flash overcomes movement of flowers blowing in the wind and softens harsh contrast at the same time, if one flash is used to simulate

115

the sun and the second is positioned to fill in the dark shadows caused by the first.

If you don't have a second flash, place a piece of aluminum foil on the side of or behind the main subject (but out of the picture space). When you point your flash at your subject, the foil will reflect the light which goes past the subject and will soften strong shadows.

Of course, aluminum foil is every bit as useful for this purpose if you're not using flash at all, but want to soften shadows caused by the sun. Foil which has been crumpled and then smoothed out again is full of wrinkles. It reflects light much more evenly than unwrinkled foil, which may produce a more direct or spotlight effect. Foil was used to lighten dark areas in the photograph on page 133. If you want to "warm" the light a little, tape in random fashion some pieces of gold foil to the aluminum. During long exposures keep moving or jiggling the reflector for even distribution of the reflected light.

Photographers who are at ease with technical data will have no trouble figuring out how to use several flash heads all at once, and indeed will take great pleasure in the exercise. But the rest of us may find the effort neither pleasant nor conducive to good mental health. There comes a point when equipment becomes physically and emotionally cumbersome. When you reach that point, look for other solutions to your problems. Don't let your equipment stand in the way of your pleasure. The best flash equipment for you is the least you can get by with, while still making the pictures you want.

Remember that the light from a flash unit does not extend to the end of the earth. You can't illuminate a whole city or landscape with it! Similarly, there's no point in trying to use an ordinary flash unit in the fortieth row of a hockey stadium. If you capture the action successfully, it will be because of the illumination from the stadium's floodlights, not because of your flash. If you're sitting in the front row (and don't have a glass shield in front of you, which will show up the flash as a hot spot in your picture), then flash will be useful for stopping the action, provided of course that the hockey players are within range of your flash, and not at the other end of the rink. Different flash units have different power. Some will cast light over much greater distances than others. These cost more and usually weigh more. You should purchase a unit which is suited to your needs.

Flash can be useful even when you have plenty of available light and don't need it for illumination. For example, if you are photographing under fluorescent lights (which often produce unpleasant colour renditions), you can get reasonably acceptable colour by bouncing light from a flash off a white wall or ceiling, because the light of a flash closely approximates daylight. Even if you still depend on the fluorescent lights as your main light source, the flash will correct the colour to a considerable degree.

You can also use flash to create shadows which will fall across an empty area, thus reducing the visual distraction. You can use flash to illuminate one part of a picture very strongly, so other elements are subdued by comparison. You can fire off a flash during a time exposure – perhaps to illuminate a passing car at night, and then continue the exposure to record the trail of headlights and tail-lights. The possibilities are endless.

However, in the vast majority of photographic situations you will not need to use flash at all. Fast films, wide apertures, reflectors, and placing your camera on a tripod are good alternatives for photographing in low light. But, if you are buying a flash, think of it as a creative tool, as a practical aid to exposure in weak illumination, and as a device for correcting colour. If you consider its many uses, you will be more likely to select the unit which will serve you well in a variety of situations.

Creating double exposures

Double exposures allow you to indulge in fantasy, but one of their strongest uses is the intensification of reality – making a snowy scene snowier, for example, or enhancing the effect of a meadow full of wildflowers. The photograph on page 156 shows the kind of effect you can get with double exposures.

Let's talk about the winter scene. Imagine the edge of a forest in a storm. Great green-black spruce trees are becoming laden with snow. Drifts are piling up around the trees, and the air is full of flakes. What you see makes you feel very "wintery," but you know the feeling won't be easy to capture on film. Try double exposure.

Set your camera on a tripod and compose your image – snowy trees and drifts which are perhaps seven to ten metres away. Focus on the trees and drifts, and shoot. (I'll explain the details later.) Then, for your second image on that same piece of film, leave the camera in exactly the same position, but refocus much closer to the camera so the nearer snowflakes seem distinct and clear. Let the background go a little out of focus. Shoot again. The result is a forest scene which seems intensely snowy. Viewers will shiver in their boots.

When spring comes, photographers flock to cherry and apple blossoms. If you're one of the people who are lured by these lovely flowers, try double exposure to express more fully the effect which they have on you. Fill the frame with branches covered with blossoms. Use maximum depth of field (f/16 or f/22) to make sure every blossom will be perfectly clear and sharp. Shoot! Then, for your second exposure, throw the entire picture out of focus in order to produce a gentle blending of pinks and whites and pale greens. Shoot again! Your final image will say "It's spring!" far more effectively than a purely documentary photograph.

Is this "creating" with your camera? Maybe, but I believe it's really recording more authentically just how you feel about cherry blossoms and spring. You capture some of your delight.

Double exposure is a very useful camera technique which we tend to ignore or forget about, because we don't take the time to figure out how it's done. Because cameras differ it's not possible to explain how everybody can make double exposures with his or her camera. Consult the instruction manual which came with your camera, or ask a photographer who's more experienced than you are.

Basically, you have to learn how to keep the film in place (not advance it to the next frame) while you cock the shutter. All that's necessary on some cameras is to press the film release button (which you do every time you rewind a roll of film) while cocking the shutter.

On other cameras you have to rewind the film by one frame, and then cock the shutter (and advance film) in the usual way. To begin with this may not be a very precise operation, and you'll find when you view your negatives or slides that you have not managed to make the second image fit exactly on top of the first. If this happens, don't panic – practise. A little more trial and error should give you almost perfect control. Don't give up because perfect alignment eludes you on your first or second attempt.

You may face a problem of another sort when making double exposures – overexposing slightly. If you have carefully calculated that $\frac{1}{30}$ second at f/11 is the proper exposure for the light available, then surely two exposures of half that amount (i.e., $\frac{1}{60}$ second at f/11), the second exposure on top of the first, will give you exactly the same results, right? Wrong! Your images may be slightly overexposed.

You must either underexpose by $\frac{1}{2}$ to $\frac{2}{3}$ of an f/stop on one of the two exposures, or by about $\frac{1}{3}$ of an f/stop on both of them. If your images are still brighter than you like, underexpose a little more. If they're not bright enough, underexpose less. Multiple exposures require a little more patience, but the principles are the same, and you can soon learn to achieve accurate exposure with practice.

Give double exposures a double try. First, learn how to make them, and second, keep on making them regularly. With this photographic technique, one idea can be linked to another in an endless series of visual adventures.

Calculating long exposures
with a through-the-lens meter

There is a quick and easy method for calculating long exposures with your
through-the-lens meter. It's rather like learning to ride a bicycle – it takes a few
minutes to catch on, but once you've got the hang of it, you can do it for life.

Let's say you're in a dark forest and you stumble across a mushroom so exquisite
that only death or lack of a meter reading will prevent you from photographing it.
All you have is the meter in your camera. So you'll have to deal with the question
of exposure, and you'll have to use the only meter you have.

When you size up the situation, you realize that you want to shoot at f/16 for
maximum depth of field. But the light is so weak that when you put your lens
opening at f/16 you get no meter reading, even if you set the shutter speed at
1 second. Here's how you solve the problem.

1 / Leave your shutter set at 1 second, and start opening your aperture from f/16
to f/11, then to f/8, f/5.6, f/4, and finally f/2.8. That's five full f/stops. If you still
can't get the needle in your meter to give a reading, stay cool. All is not lost.

2 / Leaving your shutter speed at 1 second and your lens opening at f/2.8, double
your ISO rating from, let's say ISO 25 to ISO 50. If nothing happens, double it
again to ISO 100. Now, let's assume the meter indicates that you can get a proper
exposure. So, *if* you had ISO 100 film in your camera, you could get a good
exposure at 1 second with a lens opening of f/2.8. But you don't have ISO 100 film,
and you want to make the photograph at f/16. What do you do?

3 / Just so you won't forget about it later, put the ISO dial back to 25. Then start
to calculate as follows.

By moving from f/16 to f/2.8 (five f/stops), you doubled the light five times.
That's *five doubles*. By doubling your ISO rating twice, and adding it to the five
doubles you made with the f/stops, you have *seven doubles*.

4 / To get a proper exposure at f/16 you now *double seven times* your shutter speed of

1 second. One second doubled seven times looks like this – 2 seconds, 4 seconds, 8, 16, 32, 64, 128, or about 2 minutes. Two minutes is the correct length of time to expose this shot at f/16. However, since the time is so long, reciprocity failure will affect the final result. (For an explanation of reciprocity failure, see page 45.)

5 / To overcome reciprocity failure, a/ for exposures between 4 seconds and 1 minute, add half the calculated time; b/ for exposures over 1 minute, double the calculated time. So, for a 2 minute exposure add another 2 minutes, for a final exposure of 4 minutes. Or, if you can afford to sacrifice some depth of field, open your lens one f/stop to f/11 for 2 minutes and you will get the same exposure. The effect of reciprocity failure is not as abrupt as I've implied. In other words, adding half the calculated exposure up to 1 minute and then doubling it after that is actually too arbitrary. These are guidelines, not absolute rules, and call for a little judgement. As well, add less than the recommended *extra* time of 2 minutes on a calculated exposure of 2 minutes, if you want a darker image. An exposure of 3 minutes, instead of 4 minutes, is the same as opening your lens ½ stop.

Once you've got the hang of this and practise a few times, you will never forget it. Since I prefer to use natural light rather than flash, I use the method constantly, and even though I'm not gifted in mathematics I can work out exposures in no time at all.

Making pictures at night

The beginning photographer often thinks that making pictures at night is very difficult – something which only experienced professionals should try. But that's not so. If you have a tripod, or a flash, or both, you have all the equipment you need. The rest is simply a matter of learning – and the learning is easy. Making some good pictures at night will do wonders for your ego, and will give you the confidence to try photographing other situations which you regard as difficult. So plan a little excursion for evening – soon.

Landscapes at night
In the country there's not much you can do to make a good landscape once it's pitch-black. This means that the hour between sunset and complete darkness (even on a cloudy day) is the time to do your shooting.

From about twenty minutes to about forty minutes after sunset, the sky and light are deep, rich blue – if you're facing east. From about forty minutes to one hour after sunset, you'll have the same hue if you face the western sky. It's a marvellous colour, and you must be careful not to overexpose your pictures and desaturate the blue, for if you do your scene will look wishy-washy. This is particularly true when the ground is covered with snow.

Night landscapes in winter are usually more successful than those made at other times of the year, because the snow reflects light and shows up all sorts of detail that you can't capture in summer. However, to be successful the picture should be slightly underexposed. Also, there must be a light source in the picture to contrast with the rich blue of twilight. Without a light in a window, or the moon, or the headlights of an approaching car, landscapes properly exposed to record the twilight colour and tones will look merely underexposed.

Carry a penlight after sunset so you can read the shutter speed and lens aperture dials easily. I usually calculate my exposure by opening the lens as far as it will go, say f/2.8, then reading what shutter speed will give me a normal exposure, ½ second perhaps. If I want maximum depth of field for a landscape, and I usually do, I'll open my lens to f/16, and make a time exposure, which would be 16 seconds in this situation. (See pages 120 and 121 for an explanation of how to calculate long exposures with your through-the-lens meter.) Remember that, on long exposures, a film reacts more slowly to light, and the effective film speed or ISO is reduced. So, 16 seconds at f/16 will produce a darker picture than ½ second at f/2.8. The shorter exposure will yield an image close to middle grey (middle blue, if you're using colour), but the longer exposure will produce the rich saturated colours so characteristic of early evening. Don't compensate; leave the calculated duration of the time exposure as it is.

It's possible to fake a twilight scene by shooting during the daytime, using a blue filter or tungsten film, and underexposing by about two to three stops, but the effect is not quite authentic. Besides, it's difficult to come up with a contrasting spot of yellowish light which will give the dark blue cast a real twilight feeling; however, it can be done by double exposure, if you're careful. (See "Creating double exposures," pages 118 and 119.)

The trick is either to add the moon to your "faked" evening landscape or to have it on the film before you photograph the scene. (This also applies to land-scapes actually made during the evening, but at a time when, or in a direction where, the moon is not showing.) I prefer to have moons on the film in advance. Here's how you do it.

Start with an empty camera. 1/Cock the shutter, so it will be impossible for the film advance lever to move. 2/Insert a roll of film in your camera and put the tip of the film leader in the take-up spool. 3/Advance the film by hand until the sprocket holes on both sides of the film just reach the take-up spool or some other point in the back of your camera which you won't forget. 4/Close the back of your camera, and press the shutter release. 5/Advance the film two more times, which means shooting off two more frames, something you do with every roll of film. Now you're ready to shoot a roll of moons, which you can use on a future evening.

Wait until the sky is completely black, then go out with your tripod, camera, and a lens of your choosing (probably 135mm or longer). On the first five frames, with your camera in the horizontal position, place the moon in the upper right of the picture space. On the next five frames, put it in the upper left. Switch to the vertical format and repeat the right-left exercise. Continue shooting the moon until you've finished the roll. Keep exact notes of what you've done (i.e., first five frames – horizontal format, moon in upper right). Rewind the film carefully, so you don't roll the film leader inside the cassette. Put the film into the tin it came in, wrap your notes around it, and put the film in your refrigerator to keep fresh for the evening you saunter forth to make landscapes at twilight.

What you have, of course, are 20 or 36 exposures of the moon, but on each frame, only on the spot where the image of the moon was placed, is the film actually exposed. The rest of the frame is not exposed because the sky was completely black when you photographed the moon, so you can reexpose the entire film later on – adding a landscape to each moon.

When you put the roll of moons into your camera again, you must load it exactly as before if you want the moons to appear on each frame in the spot you originally placed them. The photograph on page 138 was made by using this technique.

But what about exposing the moon properly? I've read various suggestions and found that most of them work, but try these. A full moon is quite bright, and will record perfectly by using the largest aperture at, for example, $\frac{1}{125}$ second on ISO 100 film. A half moon is not as bright, so try $\frac{1}{30}$ second. For a crescent moon, try $\frac{1}{15}$ second. (If you breathe lightly on the lens just before you make the exposure, the moon will appear to have a soft haze around it. A UV filter will protect your lens from the moisture.)

When you're photographing only the moon, there's no reason for making long exposures, such as one second or longer, because you don't require depth of field. You don't need to use anything but your widest aperture. Besides, the longer the exposure, the greater the likelihood that the moon will move slightly during the exposure and appear to be blurred or oval in shape. The only exception to this is when you're shooting a landscape in which the moon is actually present – then you may need considerable depth of field, and you'll have to try to get as much as you require without making an exposure so long that the moon will blur.

When you are calculating exposure for your landscape, don't worry about the original exposure which you gave the moon. It has no bearing whatever on the exposure required for your landscape. With night landscapes you should examine all parts of the picture area with even greater care than usual.

Remember that when the ground is bare, large sections may lack detail and appear murky or black in the final image, and you may want to reduce the amount of these areas in your composition.

Night scenes in the city
Twilight is also a good time for making night images in the city, because the sky is

not completely black and it's easy to see the outline of buildings. But, no matter how dark it is, you are always sure to have some artificial lighting.

Since the colour of lights varies tremendously, no one film can render them all accurately. Tungsten film (or daylight film with a blue filter) is more useful than daylight film, but if you don't have any tungsten film, go ahead and make pictures anyway. You'll be quite happy with the results. Daylight films simply make colours appear warmer than normal.

On rainy nights city pavements become an imperfect mirror of the lights above, a kind of psychedelic fantasy, and once you really start looking you'll see colour and patterns everywhere. Don't worry about the rain. Read my earlier suggestions for protecting your equipment, and head out with confidence.

When you're trying to determine what your exposure should be, meter carefully. For an average scene, avoid metering off the darkest areas or the brightest lights; instead, find an area of middle tone. If you can't avoid dark areas or bright lights, try to balance the size of the area which each occupies; in other words, strike an average and you won't be too far wrong on your exposure. While you should always try to underexpose night scenes, you can err quite a bit with city photographs and get away with it. Different exposures of the same scene simply give different effects.

If you don't want light trails from moving vehicles, wait for red lights to bring traffic to a halt. However, light trails imply activity and bustle, so you may want to make the longest time exposure you can in order to stretch or intensify the lines of moving lights. (This is a time when a locking cable release is useful.)

Long exposures are also excellent at fairgrounds, especially for Ferris wheels and fireworks. If you want several bursts of fireworks in one picture, make a time exposure. Simply place your hand over the lens when the first burst has faded, and keep it there until the next burst. Then, pull your hand away for a few seconds. You can repeat this several times without worrying about exposure, particularly if the sky is quite black. If the sky is rich, deep blue, make sure that your lens is set at f/16 or f/22. With these settings you can still record several bursts of fireworks without overexposing the sky.

Flash is useful at night when you want to correct the colour of objects near the lens, or if you want to prevent nearby people from being blurred. You can fire the flash as you start your time exposure, but continue the exposure to bring up detail in distant objects which the flash won't reach.

Finally, if you're afraid of prowling around the city at night by yourself, make up a small group of friends to go with you. Other photographers are best, because they won't become impatient. They'll be busy making pictures too.

Other night situations

Learn to see the darkness as an asset. Objects standing against a cluttered background can be illuminated by flash, which will eliminate or at least subdue the background. Night provides a dark stage curtain behind the actors and the set, and a photographer can take advantage of it to simplify design.

If you want to illuminate a background object, have an assistant stand near it with a slave unit. (A slave unit is a secondary flash which is triggered by the light of the main flash unit.) If you can't get an assistant, try a time exposure with a locking cable release. Flash your foreground as you press the release, and then, while you leave your camera in position on the tripod with the shutter open, move your flash unit to the second position and fire it again. If you feel so inclined, you can run to several spots and fire the flash, but after a while your picture may start to get cluttered with light. Because it's dark, you can walk through your picture without showing up on the film.

Photographing lightning is rather like making pictures of fireworks. The one prerequisite is to wait until the sky is black. All you have to do then is set your camera up on a tripod, point the lens in the direction of the lightning flashes, use the smallest aperture (f/16 or f/22), and start a time exposure. Let the exposure continue until you get one good lightning flash, or two or three minor ones. (See the photograph on page 136.) It helps to have a wide-angle lens for this, because it can cover more of the sky.

If you really want to produce a winner, have a friend stand in a raincoat about three to five metres in front of the camera (once you have some lightning on the frame) and fire off a flash gun at him. The resulting shot of a bedraggled person struggling in out of the wet, with lightning flashing all around him, will be a visual triumph, if not an artistic statement.

Twilight and night photography produce many technical and visual challenges. Don't shy away from photographing when it's dark, because you think the circumstances are too difficult for you. Give it a try. Start with something at which you think you may succeed, study the pictures you get, and try again. In this way you will increase the number of situations in which you can work with confidence, and before very long you'll be encouraging other photographers to join you.

Selective focus refers to a wide aperture (such as f/1.8 or f/3.5) used to achieve very shallow depth of field. It's a technique that demands extremely careful focusing, and it's one of the most effective ways to create points of visual emphasis while reducing the importance of surrounding material. I made this picture in a city junk yard, which was full of old cars, signs, mattresses, and what-have-you. I spent a day there finding designs in the manufactured waste. As an exercise in learning to see, it was hard to beat.

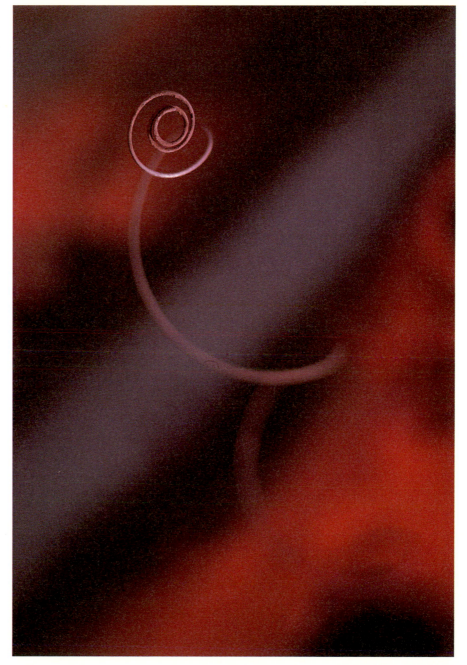

Zooming in or out with a zoom lens during an exposure can produce a dramatic sense of motion and create exciting design. I photographed these African dancers at $\frac{1}{15}$ second; my camera was on a tripod and I zoomed rapidly, commencing a split second before I released the shutter. It's useful to preview the subject area at the minimum and maximum focal lengths of the lens before you zoom, in order to determine what is likely to be in the final composition. However, even with repeated practice, the result will always be something of a surprise.

I photographed these dancers at ⅟₃₀ second, which gave them time to move considerably during the exposure. Their movement caused blur, and created a strong impression of activity. A slower speed might have conveyed the feeling of the dance even more, but I was shooting in very bright sunlight with ISO 64 film and didn't want to risk overexposing the image. A slower film (ISO 25, for example) would have allowed me to reduce the shutter speed, and for that reason would have been a better choice. I used a 300mm lens to eliminate all extraneous surrounding objects.

Panning is an especially useful technique when photographing moving objects or people. The moving object will remain basically sharp, but surrounding material will be blurred. For this picture I used ISO 25 film and a shutter speed of $\frac{1}{15}$ second in bright sunlight; a faster film would have been fine on a cloudy day. The shutter speed you choose will depend on the speed at which your subject is moving, how close you are to it, and the degree of blur you want in the surroundings; but $\frac{1}{60}$ second is usually the upper limit. If you have never panned, give it a try.

Back lighting, accurate exposure of the boy's face, and good timing were all important in taking this portrait. Instead of using fill-in flash to reduce contrast between sunlit and shadowed areas, I took advantage of the sun reflecting off the sand. I had set my camera at the reading for shade that I had metered off my hand before I started to photograph. This allowed me to get both the halo effect and facial detail. The placement of the orange in the lower corner harmonizes with the circular shape of both the face and the back-lighted fur.

The home or workplace is often a good environment to photograph people. It can enrich a visual image, as well as give viewers more information about your subject. The fishing boats and docks form a complex backdrop for this portrait, but the pattern of major lines and tones draws attention to the man. The soft light gives excellent detail to his face and reduces contrast in other areas. I was unable to use a tripod here, so the depth of field is not as great as I wanted.

A nature photographer shows his respect for a subject by providing accurate information about it in the photograph. I always use available light for mushrooms, no matter how long an exposure is required. I photographed these fungi in weak sunlight which filtered through trees to the forest floor, using a 100mm macro lens and a small piece of aluminum foil to reflect light onto the stalks and bases, which were much too dark in comparison with the caps. The camera position made it possible to show the gill structure, often an important detail in identifying mushrooms.

It's always tempting to use the longest lens available when photographing wild animals. But it's a temptation to be resisted when you want to show animals (and plants) in their natural habitat. This shot was made with a 135mm lens, and it tells a more complete story than pictures I made that day with a 300mm lens. I spent several hours near these mule deer, time enough for them to overcome their fear of me. Photographing wild animals requires time and patience. So, before you set out, it's a good idea to put some food in your pocket – for you, not for the animals.

Rain and snow can often be captured best with a slow shutter speed. Include areas of dark tone in the picture, so the drops or flakes will stand out. I recorded this snowstorm at $\frac{1}{15}$ second, but $\frac{1}{8}$ or $\frac{1}{30}$ second would have been acceptable. If the wind is strong, you'll require a speed faster than $\frac{1}{15}$ second in order to prevent the flakes from appearing as long, white streaks. If you use a flash at a faster shutter speed ($\frac{1}{60}$ second or more) you'll "freeze" the flakes and eliminate all movement. However, a flash fired during a slow exposure ($\frac{1}{15}$ or $\frac{1}{8}$ second) can give dramatic results.

I photographed this bolt of lightning with a 28mm lens on ISO 25 film. The film speed was important, because it allowed me to make time exposures lasting several minutes without worrying about overexposure. It was pure luck that the lightning flashed right where I wanted it, about ten seconds after I opened the shutter. If I had wanted several bolts in the picture, I would simply have exposed for a longer period, hoping that more lightning would strike in the same area.

When I photograph a waterfall or waves crashing on a beach, I like to capture the movement of the water, so I usually choose speeds of 1/15 second or slower. Sometimes, if the light is weak and I want to create a misty atmosphere, I'll make time exposures. The small waterfall surrounded by frozen droplets of spray was in the dark shadow of a hill, so I used 1/8 second. The slow speed makes the waterfall come alive; it makes the water flow and gives the falls a lithe and sensuous shape. None of these effects was possible at speeds of 1/125 or 1/250 second.

It's almost impossible to record a landscape in late twilight and a rising moon at the same time. If you expose for the moon, you'll underexpose the scene. If you expose for the scene, you'll overexpose the moon. Besides, the moon seldom rises exactly where you want it in your composition. The best solution is double exposure, the technique I used here. I shot a roll of moons and kept the unprocessed film in the refrigerator, hoping to use it again during a trip through northern Ontario. One afternoon I saw this church at Longlac, and decided to come back at twilight. Before I returned, I loaded my camera with the film which already had a moon on every frame. All I had to do was to add the scene.

Photographing children and other people

Once I unexpectedly met a friend of mine at the Y.W.C.A. She was crawling across the floor on her hands and knees, with a camera hanging around her neck and 30 four-year-olds in tow. Everybody was having a ball! Suddenly she stopped, turned around, and shouted, "Hey, don't we make a great snake!" By the time all the kids had stopped yelling their agreement at the top of their lungs, she had five or six pictures of them, and the snake was slithering on down the hall and into the gym.

This woman is the best photographer of children I've ever met. She always has her camera with her, so the kids never notice it. She's photographed them as giraffes, leprechauns, and trees. She's caught them plunging their hands into chocolate cake and crying over spilled milk. She's made pictures of them dressing up, talking on the phone, and having fights.

Her pictures are good because she's never forgotten what it's like to be a child. She knows how important it is to pretend, and to cry when you're sad and laugh when you're happy. Children love her. They even come in off the street and ask to have their picture taken. If they want to dress up, she'll haul out a carton full of oversized and outlandish clothes, and let them go to it. She photographs them while they're dressing, and after they say, "I'm all ready now" – when they pose very deliberately indeed.

Photographing children
Good pictures of children are made by adults who meet kids on their own ground, but seldom by people who try it the other way around. If you start off by lining children up or by making them sit down in front of a camera, you can count yourself lucky if you get one good photograph. So why fight the odds? Play with them, and let your picture-making be a game.

It's important visually to photograph children wherever they happen to be, assuming the situation is of their choosing. Imposed circumstances are revealed by tenseness, stiffness, and apprehension in a child's face or body. It's just about as important to toss every preconceived idea of composition out the window, and let what children are doing become your guiding principle. Don't worry about rules like "a person should be running into the picture space, not out of it," because it's common for kids to chase each other, and having a child near the edge of the picture and heading out may suggest a successful escape. Try to adopt a mental attitude which is as loose and free as that of the children you're photographing.

There's a good deal to be said for shooting sequences of children. Try for that one great shot, sure, but keep in mind that a series of slides or prints will probably make a more complete story, and will give added delight to the people who see them.

You'll probably be able to make sequences more easily if you depend entirely on available light, and if you keep your equipment to a minimum. Don't weigh yourself down. Select an appropriate lens, such as a 50mm, 100mm, or 135mm, and start off with a new roll of film, so you can count on a good session of shooting before you have to change rolls.

Sequences permit the use of many different techniques to convey children's activity, such as panning, blurring, and recording peak action. Sequences permit you to explore many points of view, from long-distance environmental shots to extreme close-ups. But most of all, sequential shooting encourages visual freedom and a variety of interpretations.

After you have your photographs processed, treat the children to your first slide show or exhibition of prints. Let them react to what you've done. They won't give you much in the way of visual instruction, but they will let you know by their laughter and silence which pictures mean the most to them. You won't get this sort of evaluation from anyone else, and yet it is perhaps the most useful instruction of all – kids telling adults what's good and what isn't. The children's response will help you to revise your photo story, and make you more perceptive the next time you photograph kids.

Making candids

Most of the ideas you have for photographing children can be used when you make pictures of grown-ups, but the chances are that you'll be making more posed photographs of adults and fewer candids. The distinction between candid and posed pictures is a useful one, because the different circumstances offer different challenges, and tend to yield very different results.

Let's consider candid pictures first. A candid photograph is one for which the subject does not prepare, although the photographer must. Good candid pictures of people don't just happen. How can you prepare? Here are some suggestions.

1 / If you have two camera bodies, put a standard lens on one and a 100mm or a 135mm or a zoom on the other; if you have just one camera, choose the lens you find easiest to work with. Hang your camera or cameras around your neck – this is one time you can forget about your tripod.

2 / When you arrive at the shooting location, choose the shutter speed you expect to use for most of your pictures, and set your cameras at that speed, let's say $\frac{1}{125}$ second. (This is also a departure from usual practice; normally you choose a lens opening first.)

3 / Once you've set the shutter speed, determine which lens openings you will need for sunny situations and for shade, perhaps f/11 and f/5.6. You can do this by metering off your hand both in the shade and the sun (fill the frame with your hand). An aperture of at least f/5.6 is necessary for full-frame portraits made with a 100mm lens or longer, because it will ensure that both nose and eyes are sharp if you focus on the cheekbone. Medium depth of field gives you a margin for error in focusing, especially useful when you have to shoot fast. Establishing basic exposure settings before you make pictures means that you can shoot without worrying about changing shutter and lens-opening dials, or at most that all you will have to do is change quickly from the one lens opening to the other.

4 / Be open about your picture making. Let people see you. That way you'll have far more opportunities than if you try to sneak around or hide. If anybody doesn't want to be photographed, he or she will either tell you or move away. Everybody else will soon ignore you. Then it's easy to shoot. If people start to pose for you when you don't want them to, waste three or four pictures. Most people, especially children, will start to relax by then, and will stop posing.

Good candid photographs of people are usually a result of good timing. You anticipate a particular moment or activity, or a configuration of elements in which a person becomes central to a strong visual design, or a significant expression or gesture – and you release the shutter at the moment when everything is right. Some photographers are especially gifted at sensing an important moment, and their photographs are records not merely of what people are doing, but of who they are and what they are feeling. It's a sensitivity which can be developed. Remember that it's the significant expression or moment which counts, so don't be unduly concerned if an extraneous element appears in a corner, or if somebody's foot is cut off.

A good exercise is to return to a situation several times, especially after you've seen the results of your first shooting. Most communities offer many opportunities to do this. Perhaps there's a senior citizens' group which meets regularly, or daily hockey practices in a nearby arena, or a busy local market. Start by photographing in situations where you feel comfortable, and as you gain confidence you'll find it easier to photograph people with whom you are not familiar, but who intrigue, stimulate, or puzzle you. In this way photography will increase your understanding of others and will become an even greater challenge – visually and emotionally.

Making posed pictures
Posed photographs, unlike candids, require preparation of both the model and the photographer, and can usually be classified as either formal or informal. A formal picture of a person is one in which the model and his surroundings are strictly arranged by the photographer, often according to a preconceived design. For an informal picture, the model is given general instructions only and responds to the photographer and the surroundings with considerable freedom, while the photographer shoots. In both types of pictures the model is fully aware of the camera and is participating in the making of the picture; but in informal shooting the model creates or directs the image just as much as the photographer does. The photographer, however, chooses when to shoot, and must recognize the best moments.

The challenge of making posed pictures of either a formal or an informal nature is partly in the relationship which you establish with your subject. It's important that both of you be at ease, if you hope to make images which reveal some aspect of the model's character, personality, or mood. But outstanding posed pictures usually go beyond the recording of one individual on film, and express something universal about people. Such pictures are rare, but they are a standard to seek, because the effort will improve every picture you make.

When you pose a model for a formal close-up portrait, you are making the model's eyes the most important visual element, especially if you are shooting with black-and-white film. With colour film, certain hues or the intensity of colours can divert a viewer's attention to the lips or the clothes, both of which are usually of much less significance. So, you must be careful to avoid visual conflicts.

In close-up portraits it's usually best to show the dark side of the face, reducing the area that contains highlights. Try placing the brightest highlights in the eyes.

The placement of the model's eyes in the picture space is important. A central placement suggests rigidity. Placement above the centre of the picture area is often the best choice when you are using the vertical format, and to one side or the other when you are using the horizontal format. The direction in which the model is looking will also influence the interpretation. Downcast eyes suggest embarrassment, modesty, or sadness. Eyes which are looking up suggest anticipation, excitement, or pleasure. Seldom should both eyes of the model be on the same horizontal plane, because this reduces the sense of vitality. In order to overcome a static arrangement of the eyes, give the camera a slight tilt so the model will appear to be looking up. Don't ask your model to tilt her head, because it may be awkward for her, and if so it will show.

You should avoid horizontal lines in a portrait in most cases, although there certainly are exceptions, and also strong vertical lines, especially if they lead to the bottom of the picture area and take your eyes out of the picture. Pay careful attention to the lines formed by the shoulders and arms. Oblique lines are dynamic lines, and enhance the feeling of life. Usually shoulders and arms can be used to create obliques which bring a dynamic quality to the picture.

Above all, remember that lines, colours, tones, and other elements of composition are strongly influenced by the quality of light and the direction of lighting. Diffused light will establish a gentle mood and reduce contrast; strong side lighting will reveal the texture of the skin and introduce bold shadows. Try to use the elements of design and other photographic controls in ways that harmonize with the personality of your model. Since models differ, your techniques and compositions must vary.

Informal portraits are more difficult than formal ones in one respect – the photographer has less control over the model. But this lack of control has many compensations. Chief among these is the naturalness which the model shows, so the photographer needs to spend much less time and effort overcoming stiffness or nervousness. The informal approach is good for photographing people in their middle years. The very young and very old are relatively unconcerned about their appearance and status, but most adults worry about these things and are sometimes quite difficult to pose. If you can photograph them while they are talking to you or to somebody else, and thereby avoid having to pose them, you'll probably get better results.

A basic principle of portraiture, formal or informal, is to seek unity of impression between the visual elements and the model's expression. Try to determine the centre of interest before you shoot. Is it the eyes, the whole face, a certain kind of expression, or even the clothing? Beyond that, be flexible. Avoid specific formulas. The suggestions I've given you are intended as useful guides, not as rules. You must change them or ignore them when you feel your subject or the specific moment requires it.

One way to avoid stereotyped portraits is to photograph your subjects in their own environments – a truck driver leaning against the cab of his truck, a cook surrounded by shelves of spices, a woodcutter in the forest. The habitat will do more than provide information; it will add visual and psychological dimension to your pictures of people if you regard it as important, and not as merely another prop.

There's also a reverse approach which is a lot of fun, and which can often reveal a good deal about your model. Pose your subject in a situation which most people would think of as contradictory – a nurse in her white uniform sitting on a big, black motorcycle; a leather-jacketed motorcyclist cuddling a baby; an elderly woman swinging a baseball bat. This approach is not as frivolous as it may seem. When people are placed in unfamiliar circumstances, they have to respond in terms of their past experiences, or behave in ways which they think are expected of them, or react with confusion. How they react frequently creates first-rate opportunities for making photographs.

The most satisfying photographs of people usually result from close personal feelings between the subject and the photographer. That's why mothers who know how to use a camera often make the best pictures of their children. It's also why going back to a situation again and again is so important. Repeated visits seldom exhaust the photographic potential; in fact, familiarity is essential to perception and understanding and makes more and better pictures possible. Photographing people is one way to make good pictures – and good friends.

It's important to be yourself when you are making pictures. Don't be intimidated by formulas or rules – or elephants in any guise. Photograph the things that matter to you. Whenever possible, analyse your response to the subject matter before making technical decisions about your equipment. Sometimes you'll have to act fast, as I did here, so experience is valuable. The way to gain experience is to make photographs. For the picture I used an 85 – 200mm zoom lens, shooting as close as I could get to the ground, in order to place the elephant against the sky and increase the sense of its size.

This photograph is essentially a careful balance of colours and shapes. The red and white pole has neither a top nor a base, and is physically unrelated to the house. Nevertheless, I thought the juxtaposition of the pole and the building made a compelling design. Good picture possibilities exist everywhere, and unpromising situations should be regarded as visual challenges.

A picture which required a
familiarity with hens! The only
thing which wasn't planned was the
placement of the egg, which had
been carelessly dropped by one of
the birds. To get the effect of a hen
looking at the egg lying in such an
unusual spot, I had to make sure it
paused as it came through the door.
Since a hen sees better to either
side than it does to the front, I
placed my tripod to one side of the
door, knowing that any hen that
poked its head out would stop
immediately when it saw me. Six
individual hens had emerged
before these three suddenly
appeared together.

This is neither a double exposure nor two slides sandwiched together, but the result of simple observation. A partly-opened window picked up the reflection of the sunset to the right of the picture area. Through the glass I could see the houses and the mountain beyond. I set up my tripod inside the room and used a 135mm lens at f/22, focusing on a point beyond the glass but in front of the buildings. A slight lack of sharpness in the clouds seemed to increase the dreamlike effect, but I made certain the background was fully in focus.

Rainy nights are ideal times for photographing a city, simply because wet pavement reflects coloured lights so well. This fantasy of Toronto's city hall was made in a series of puddles. Exposure was difficult because of large black areas, so once I had a good idea of what my composition would be, I removed the camera from the tripod and crouched down to meter only off the reflections. A hand-held meter would have been simpler to use. Yes, the picture *is* upside down. I'm interested in the effect, not the reality.

Visual incongruities are often arresting. The little girl in the black uniform seems out of place among the brightly-coloured beach houses. One wonders why she is there. The question is the reason for the image. I used a 300mm lens to eliminate peripheral details and to compress distance while emphasizing lines and shapes. The black figure contains the only important curved lines in the picture and, for this reason, as well as the absence of colour in her clothes, is clearly the centre of interest. The picture also demonstrates the effectiveness of setting a small object in a large context.

Wide-angle lenses produce the greatest sense of depth when the camera is positioned vertically, when there is a significant foreground object, and when the lens is set for maximum depth of field. But of the three, a strong foreground is the most important. Most of the time, especially in the vertical position, the camera will need to be tilted down sharply in order to emphasize the foreground, as I have done in this picture. Less often, the lens can be used just as effectively if it is tilted up sharply to eliminate almost all the land, putting the major emphasis on the sky.

While sunlight produces texture and sparkle in snow pictures, this is no reason to put your camera away on cloudy winter days. Diffused light eliminates most of the tones in the snow, and makes it a perfect canvas for other tones and hues. On both sunny and cloudy days it's easy to underexpose snow, which makes it look grey. The solution is to take a meter reading off the snow and then open up the lens one to one and a half f/stops. This puts the white back into the snow. Every year I grow a patch of these colourful cabbages for the sole purpose of photographing them in the late fall and early winter.

Melted frost on these cabbage leaves looks like dewdrops. The cloudy weather produced a variety of tones with good highlights, but no sharp contrasts. I used a 100mm macro lens (on a tripod) and a lens opening of about f/8, which was sufficient to keep the edges of the leaves and the closest drops fully in focus. The slightest alteration of camera position or focus creates new opportunities. The possibilities can interest me for hours.

The photographs on these two pages are close-ups of out-of-focus drops of water on the same leaf. For this picture I positioned the camera above the leaf and looked down at it. For the other I placed the camera near the tip and looked along the leaf. I was using an 85 – 200mm zoom lens with an extension tube behind the lens and a close-up lens on the front. I set the aperture as wide as possible, f/4, then underexposed by shooting at $\frac{1}{1000}$ second instead of $\frac{1}{250}$ second, which the meter indicated. The widest lens opening was necessary in order to make the out-of-focus water drops appear as circles or ovals.

Pictures like these demonstrate the remarkable variety of visual opportunities available to any photographer, anywhere. You don't have to travel to faraway places to experience the joy of photography. You can find it in your own backyard. Different close-up equipment will produce different effects, so you should use whatever you have. Many close-ups, and certainly these, are impossible to previsualize. You have to poke your lens and close-up attachments into wet grass and start looking. As with the cabbages and other close-up subjects, the tiniest shift in camera position or focus can utterly change what you see in the viewfinder.

To my mind, the important question is why I made this image, not how. The reason for an image should be clear before the making. To see the moon rising out of flames makes me think of the four elements – earth, air, fire, and water – and puts me in touch with the immensity and mystery of the universe. So I photographed the lines of a prairie fire at night, and then repositioned the camera to add the moon by using double exposure. Photography is a good way to explore yourself and your place in the scheme of things. Try to understand your personal responses to different subjects – those you photograph, and those you avoid. Then the techniques you use will make sense.

Fifty tips

Over the years you will read or hear about various tips that will not only help you make the images you want, but also guide you in the use of your photographs, both personally and commercially. Keep a record of these. They can be very useful. Here are some I have found worth recording.

1 / If you are in doubt about the order of the steps to follow when making a photograph, keep the letters C, D, E in mind – in their alphabetical order. C = composition, D = depth of field, E = exposure. More often than not, you should attend to things in this order.

2 / If you are making pictures on a bright, sunny day and know the ISO rating of your film, but your light meter is not working, here's how to determine the shutter speed and aperture to use. Set your lens opening at f/16; for front and side lighting the shutter speed will always be similar to the ISO rating of the film, no matter what film you are using. For example, if your film is ISO 64 and the sun is shining, your shutter speed will be $\frac{1}{60}$ at f/16; with a film of ISO 25, your shutter speed will be $\frac{1}{30}$ second at f/16. If you don't want to use that shutter speed, you can change it, but you will know the proper combination of shutter speed and aperture.

3 / If you need a faster film than the one you have, you may arbitrarily push the ISO rating of a film and compensate by special processing. (Many labs provide special processing at extra cost.) ISO 64 film may be shot at ISO 125 or 250, for example. As a rule, don't push film more than two stops (i.e., quadruple the ISO rating). Film may also be pulled; that is, if you shoot a fast film at a slower ISO rating, you can compensate in the processing. Be sure to give the lab the rating. Avoid pushing or pulling Kodachrome films, as the processing service is often not readily available for them.

4 / If you have a fast film in your camera, and the light is so bright that you can't close down your lens as far as you want, use your polarizing filter or a neutral density filter to reduce the amount of light reaching the film.

5 / If you discover, halfway through a roll of film, that you have been using the wrong ISO rating, don't correct your mistake. Finish the entire roll at the wrong ISO. Then, when you take the film to the laboratory for processing, tell them about your error. They can compensate in the processing and save the film. This applies to both black-and-white and colour films, except for Kodachromes. If you change from the wrong ISO to the correct one part way through the roll, you will sacrifice all the pictures you made before you corrected the ISO.

6 / Photographers sometimes overexpose pictures made with telephoto or zoom lenses. If you find this happening, increase the ISO rating of your film when using one of these lenses. A film rated at ISO 64 might be adjusted to ISO 80 or 100. You are not actually changing the ISO rating of the film, you are merely fooling the lens and the light meter a little. Return to the normal ISO rating for your standard or wide-angle lens.

7 / Slides that are underexposed, but still have a recognizable image, may be useful in slide sequences. Often a photo-story builds toward a night sequence, and viewers will accept an underexposed slide as being correctly exposed if it is included in the right place.

8 / It's easy to sandwich two slides together by removing both of them from their mounts and putting them together in a single mount. Photographers have been using this technique for years to add sunsets to dull scenes or a bird to an empty sky. However, there are many unexplored possibilities for sandwiching, especially in the field of colour abstracts. Start experimenting with slightly overexposed slides which are not related in subject matter, but which may make interesting colour and design combinations. With the ideas you get, you can begin shooting pictures deliberately for sandwiching. Your purpose will be to make composite photographs which are compelling images when they are mounted and shown as one picture.

9 / If you find yourself fussing over pictures, or simply spending far too much time finding something you want to photograph, set yourself an assignment. Give yourself exactly 5 minutes to make 5 photographs. Then speed it up; give yourself

5 minutes to make 10 photographs. You can choose a specific subject in advance, if you want, such as 10 abstracts, or 10 shots of a particular meadow. This exercise is a remarkably good way to zero in on the essentials of making a picture.

10 / If you find that you are always photographing the same subject from the same point of view, deliberately set yourself the assignment of looking at the subject in different ways. For example, instead of trying to obtain lighting and detail in all parts of a person's face when shooting a portrait, try a series in which the person's face is illuminated entirely from one side. Or, instead of looking at a spider's web only from the front, try looking at it from the side.

11 / Many photographers look for reflections of colours in calm lakes and ponds; but look in moving water too. You won't find definable shapes, but you will find streaks and masses of flowing colour. Usually, the lower your camera position is the more likely you are to pick up these colours.

12 / One way to improve your ability to make good compositions is to disregard the subject matter and its meaning, and to look at your material purely as graphic design. Pay special attention to the size, placement, and light value of every tone in the picture space, whether you are using black-and-white or colour.

13 / Christmas lights can create marvellous effects. By moving in close and throwing foreground lights out of focus, you will get overlapping circles of colour, which add mystery and merriment to Christmas scenes. If you breathe lightly on your lens or filter before releasing the shutter, you will produce an aura or glow around each light. You can see the effect through your viewfinder and make the exposure immediately or as the mist on the lens starts to evaporate.

14 / If you have an image in your viewfinder which you really like, shoot two or more identical exposures. It's less expensive than having duplicates of the slides made, and the quality will be better.

15 / Fill-in flash is as useful on a bright, winter day as it is at any other time. For example, you can use it to show detail in dark objects which you are photographing against the sun. The snow may act as a reflector and bounce light into shadow areas, but if it doesn't, and you are confronted with very strong contrast, use your flash.

16 / When you are making a portrait and need some light reflected on your mod-

el's face, give the subject a book, a newspaper, or white paper to hold as if reading it. This may provide the light you require. Ideally, the paper should not appear in your picture.

17 / Putting a white handkerchief over a flash diffuses and reduces the illumination. One layer reduces light by one f/stop, two layers by two f/stops. You can hold the handkerchief on with an elastic band.

18 / If you are photographing in a room which is lighted entirely by tungsten or fluorescent bulbs, and you do not have the proper films or filters available to correct the colour rendition, consider overexposing your film slightly. This will desaturate the colours, and make unpleasant colour effects less pronounced.

19 / When shooting through glass, you can avoid reflections if you fit your lens with a flexible rubber lens hood. By placing the hood against the glass, you will eliminate annoying highlights and unwanted colours reflected in the window. If you do this with long telephoto lenses, take care to have the lens perpendicular to the glass, or distortion may occur.

20 / Many self-timers can be used to provide a fixed time exposure of a few seconds. Put the time dial to "B," and activate the self-timer. The shutter will remain open for a set time. Different makes of cameras have different exposure times. This information can be particularly useful when you are working in very low light and require this exposure time.

21 / When making nature close-ups, the easiest way to remove small distracting objects is to cover them up with material indigenous to the area. For example, if a small piece of birchbark is wedged among fallen brown leaves, simply use another leaf to cover it. Keep your picture authentic; don't cover the birchbark with a fern frond, just because you like ferns.

22 / Sometimes it is virtually impossible to photograph a flower which droops or hangs down, such as a bluebell or a pitcher plant, especially the centre of the flower. To overcome the problem, try using a mirror. Place the mirror on the ground underneath the flower, and shoot into the mirror. The blossom will probably have the sky as a background. If the centre of the flower is too dark, you can use a reflector to bounce light into the centre of the flower, and still shoot your picture by aiming your camera at the mirror.

23 / You can usually photograph moving objects that are fastened at one end, such as a waving fern, at slower shutter speeds than unattached objects moving at the same speed. (If you want to arrest motion entirely.)

24 / When hunting wild animals with a camera, there is usually little point in trying to stay hidden. Allow the animals to see you, as you move slowly, cautiously, and indirectly toward them. Always avoid swift or jerky movements. If you have enough patience, you may even be able to walk among them in the end. When camouflage is essential, wear patterned clothing, not solid colours. Some animals are attracted by unusual actions, because their curiosity is aroused. Allowing a white handkerchief to flutter in the breeze has been known to attract deer and pronghorn, for example. Other animals are curious about humans crawling on their hands and knees.

25 / You can reverse a short or normal lens to get a close-up lens of good quality. Most camera manufacturers have a reversing ring or adaptor available for their mounting method. Of course, when you reverse the lens, it loses its automatic diaphragm coupling, and you must use it as a manual lens.

26 / If the legs of your tripod will not spread far enough apart to let you make close-ups near the ground, get a small clamp which will fit the leg of a tripod, onto which you can screw the ball-and-socket head. Then, simply put your camera on the clamp and head, and make your picture.

27 / If you wear eyeglasses, you may have a problem seeing the entire picture in your viewfinder, you may have difficulty focusing (with or without your glasses), or you may find that your light meter is affected by light coming in through the eyepiece of the viewfinder – simply because your glasses prevent you from getting close enough to the eyepiece to eliminate it. If any of these is a problem, consider a visit to your optometrist and to your camera store to have a correctional lens fitted to the eyepiece of the camera viewfinder.

28 / It makes sense to have two camera bodies – for several reasons. (Be sure your lenses will fit both cameras.) Two bodies will allow you to shoot colour and black-and-white film at the same time, or a fast and a slow film. Two bodies mean less switching of lenses. A second body also means that you won't have to suspend your photographic activities when one is being repaired or serviced.

29 / If you want to reduce the possibility of your photographic equipment being stolen, use an inconspicuous camera bag, such as a flight bag. Also, don't put decals of photographic societies on your camera bag or car window.

30 / If you contemplate selling or trading in your cameras or other equipment, keep them in good condition. They will be worth more that way. However, you should always exercise reasonable care.

31 / To keep rain or snow off your camera, put it in a plastic bag which has a hole cut out for the lens.

32 / Lightweight plastic rainpants are excellent photographic gear for wet days, and make kneeling in the grass easier than using a rubber or plastic sheet, which is often a bother to carry around.

33 / If you travel in a car that has separate or bucket seats, you can secure your camera or camera bag against bumps or falls by looping the strap around the back of the seat.

34 / On a hike, an easy way to carry extra lenses is to put them in their cases and loop them onto your belt. Extra rolls of film can be carried in the same way.

35 / A hard-boiled egg will fit quite nicely into an empty film box. Keep this in mind when you want to carry a light lunch with you.

36 / If you keep losing cable releases, tie a red ribbon on your new one. When you misplace it, at least it will be easier to find. However, why not tie a string around the middle of your cable release and tie the other end of the string to your tripod? If your cable release comes unscrewed from the camera, you won't lose it.

37 / Empty aluminum foil and plastic wrap boxes make excellent storage containers for 35mm slides. You may have to reinforce the outside of the box with thin cardboard to provide a little more stiffness.

38 / Every photographer should devise a system for cataloguing negatives or slides which suits him. Once you have one, don't start cataloguing your pictures of several years ago, because the chances are that you will never catch up. Start with your new photographs and immediately catalogue every box of slides or roll of

negatives you shoot. Then, as you have time, start working backwards to catalogue your pictures from previous years.

39 / You can use your enlarger for photocopying. Remove the head of the
enlarger, affix a ball-and-socket head or another device to hold your camera, turn
the focus knob for the correct height, and add two high-intensity or flood lamps at
45-degree angles. This method can be used to copy maps, old photos, title slides,
and so on.

40 / By dipping a toothpick in undiluted bleach, you can write a title on a transparency. The bleach removes the colour, leaving white letters on the slide. Work
on the *emulsion* side of the transparency.

41 / Sometimes colour slides have tiny distracting highlights that you want to
eliminate. If the highlights are surrounded by relatively dark areas, the easiest way
to remove them is with a needle or a straight pin. Take the pin and make
extremely small circular scratches on the distracting highlights. You must do this
on the *shiny*, or *non-emulsion* side of the transparency. The tiny scratches roughen
the surface of the slide, and prevent projected light from passing directly through
it. Thus, the light is scattered and the highlights appear darkened. While you must
work over a light box as you make the scratches, you will have to project the slide
to see how effective your effort is. Practise with a few worthless slides first.

42 / Take a bulb from your projector along to a hardware store, and find a piece of
rubber hose which will fit over the bulb and grip it nicely. If you buy about 15
centimetres of hose, and carry it along with your projector wherever you take it,
you will find it very handy if a bulb burns out. By slipping the hose over the hot
bulb, you can remove it from the projector immediately and waste no time waiting for it to cool.

43 / When preparing a slide essay or sequence, avoid visual monotony by inter-
mixing verticals with horizontals, close-ups with medium- and long-distance
shots, front lighting with side and back lighting – and so on. A slide sequence will
flow most easily if each succeeding photograph contains a point of similarity
(colour, object, idea, etc.) with the preceding picture, while introducing differences. If you lay out your essay on a light box, you can easily spot weak or
ineffective transitions.

163

44 / If you have two projectors, you can project slides on two screens simultaneously. Photograph and arrange your essays with both screens in mind. For example, you can hold a picture of a field of flowers on one screen, while showing close-ups of individual flowers on the other. You can change slides one screen at a time, so the audience is never sitting in the dark; or you can change both slides at once, when you want to relieve the visual pattern or produce a more dramatic effect. Let your imagination go to work on the possibilities.

45 / If you enjoy showing slides with music, never underestimate the capacity of your audience to appreciate a wide variety of musical forms. For example, people who normally listen only to country and western music will respond with pleasure to a Bach concerto, if it is in harmony with your photographs. Music may also be used as a background for live or taped commentary, but using music, words, and slides together in a single effective presentation takes considerable skill. Start with slides and music, or slides and words, and introduce the third element only when you feel fully at ease with the other two.

46 / Every original artistic work is automatically protected by copyright from the moment of its creation. Original artistic works include photographs. Thus, no formalities are necessary to copyright a photograph in Canada, and this copyright is automatically valid in most countries. To be protected after publication, you must place a copyright symbol, the year, and your name on all copies available to the public. In Canada, protection for photographs by copyright is for fifty years from the moment the photograph is published.

47 / The owner of the copyright for a photograph is the person who owns the original negative or transparency. Usually this is the photographer. However, photographs made on assignment or commission belong to the person or firm granting the assignment, unless otherwise specified in writing. For example, if somebody commissions you to make his portrait and agrees to purchase it on completion, the copyright does not belong to you, but to the person who commissioned you, even if you retain possession of the original negatives.

48 / When you sell a photograph, you do *not* sell the copyright. The only way you can transfer copyright is by a statement in writing. You can assign (transfer) copyright in whole or in part, subject to any restrictions you want. It's very important to be specific in assigning copyright. You can specify a stated period of time, a given geographical area, a particular medium or vehicle of reproduction. (For

example, one-time reproduction rights to two photographs of grain elevators at Minnedosa, Manitoba; to be published in the annual calendar of Western Grain Growers; the year; for distribution in Manitoba, Saskatchewan, and Alberta only.) You can be less specific and assign the buyer all North American rights, or all Canadian rights for a certain period of time, or simply all rights. The greater the rights you sell, the higher your selling price should be.

49 / If you intend to have a photograph published, consider whether or not you need a model release from the people who are in the photograph. As a general rule, you may photograph a street or other public area or anything without gaining permission from people in the picture. However, if one or just a few people are singled out, written permission must be granted by the individual(s) if your photograph is to be used in advertising matter – unless the person is a celebrity and has, as a result, surrendered that part of his right to privacy. If the photograph is used as a matter of public interest, as in a newspaper, and concerns something the public has a right to be informed about and is used in just that way, the public's right takes precedence over that of the individual. Remember though that the law defends everyone against defamation. If a photograph defames a person's character, either through the image itself or in the way it is used by a publisher or advertiser, the photographer may be liable along with all others involved. A photograph that represents bare comment or illustrates a proven fact cannot be called defamation.

50 / Membership in camera clubs, photographic societies, and national photographic organizations, such as Canada's National Association for Photographic Art and the Photographic Society of America, can be valuable. Usually the small membership fee will be paid back in a very short time in what you learn.

Index

ABOUT THE AUTHOR

Freeman Patterson's interest in photography began in childhood, even though he was twenty before he could afford his first camera. That was in 1958. Since that time his involvement with photography has grown steadily.

Freeman was born at Long Reach, New Brunswick, graduated with a B.A. in philosophy from Acadia University in Nova Scotia in 1959, and received a master's degree in divinity from Union Theological Seminary at Columbia University in New York in 1962. The title of his master's thesis was "Still Photography as a Medium of Religious Expression." During his three years in New York he studied photography with Dr. Helen Manzer.

In 1965 after teaching religious studies for three years at Alberta College in Edmonton, Freeman resigned his teaching position to devote full time to photography. Since 1965 his photographs have been published in numerous books, magazines, journals, newspapers, and advertisements, and have been exhibited around the world. Many of his photographs were selected for the National Film Board's three award-winning books, *Canada: A Year of the Land, Canada*, and *Between Friends/Entre Amis*. He is the author of other acclaimed books: *Photography and the Art of Seeing, Photography of Natural Things, Namaqualand: Garden of the Gods*, and *Portraits of Earth*; and photographer for *In a Canadian Garden*.

Among the many awards and honours Patterson has received are the gold medal for distinguished contribution to photography from Canada's National Association for Photographic Art, a Doctorate of Letters from the University of New Brunswick, the gold medal for photographic excellence from the National Film Board of Canada, and the highest award (Hon EFIAP) of the Fédération Internationale de l'Art Photographique (Berne, Switzerland). He has been made a member of the Royal Canadian Academy of Art, a fellow of the Photographic Society of America, and an Honorary Fellow of the Photographic Society of Southern Africa. In 1985 he was awarded the Order of Canada.

From his home at Shampers Bluff in rural New Brunswick, Patterson travels and lectures frequently in Canada, United States, and abroad, sponsored by photographic, environmental, and educational groups.